HOLIDAY COOKING
FOR ALL
OCCASIONS

Presented By
Home Economics Teachers

Edited By
Gerry Murry Henderson

Graphics By
Robert Knies Design, Inc.

© Library of Congress Catalog
Card No. 83-072747
ISBN 0-914159-09-7

© California Cookbook Company
1907 Skycrest Drive, Fullerton, California 92631

Holiday Cooking For All Occasions

Americans love holidays – including myself! Usually it means no school, a "day off", and most often, cooking "something special" for family and good friends.

For about fifteen years now, we have worked closely with California Home Economics Teachers towards publishing quality cookbooks, a different one each year. Not only have these teachers been to college to study cooking, they also teach "life-skills" such as parenting, child care and surviving "on your own".

To all these teachers who have dedicated their lives to students, who continue to be professionals in spite of budget cuts and sometimes harsh criticism, I say THANK YOU. Not just for making these books possible, but most of all, for your inspiration and your example to me and others.

Malcolm Forbes said "The purpose of education is to replace an EMPTY mind with an OPEN mind". And the longer I am associated with inspirational teachers like yourselves, the more I understand what Forbes meant.

Further "thank yous" are in order for our annual editor, GERRY MURRY HENDERSON (who teaches at Temple City High School), who carefully edits each and every recipe, and also NANCY FREEMAN, our new Office Manager, who receives, proofs, and records all recipes as they come in. DOUG HERREMA, our Director of Publications, continues to improve our books each year with creative topics and choice photographs. THANKS DRH! DOUG PIERCE is directly responsible for the contribution of more teachers' recipes than any one of us! THANKS WDP, for your travels and your polite manners!

Several professional printers and graphic artists deserve credit (for this book and several others): ROBERT KNIES of Knies Design, Inc. in Fullerton, for art work and design; BOB CLEMENSEN and JOHN CHURCH of Associated Typographers in Anaheim; and JERRY BERNSTEIN of KNI, Inc. in Anaheim, for a quality printing job.

RUSS HERREMA, BILL HORTON, and BILL O'BRIEN continue to deliver and pick-up books all over California, and are "my main men"! We all thank them for being always dependable!

If you happen to be reading this, it's probably because you purchased one of these cookbooks from a student – selling them as a fund-raiser for their school. And YOUR PURCHASE deserves a big THANK YOU from ALL OF THE ABOVE and many more, for the multiple jobs you help create, and for supporting your local schools and children.

Sincerely,

Grady W. Reed, Owner
California Cookbook Company

P.S. PLEASE NOTE THE REORDER PAGE IN THE BACK!

CONTENTS

On Our Front Cover:
"Black Forest Chocolate Cheesecake", recipe on pg. 83 and
"Chocolate Cherry Minicakes", recipe on pg. 83,
compliments of Hershey Foods Corporation.

COLOR PHOTOGRAPHY CREDITS

Courtesy of:

Best Foods, Inc., Englewood Cliffs, New Jersey
California Poultry Industry, Modesto, California
Hershey Foods Corp., Hershey, Pennsylvania
National Broiler Council, Columbia, South Carolina
National Livestock & Meat Board, Chicago, Illinois
Pillsbury Company, Minneapolis, Minnesota

CALIFORNIA HOME ECONOMICS
TEACHERS ADVISORY COMMITTEE

Anderson, Jill
Santa Paula High School, Santa Paula

Banicevich, Gerry
Cordova Sr. High School,
Rancho Cordova

Black-Eacker, Ellen
Nogales High School, La Puente

Blass, Sue, retired
Valhalla High School, El Cajon

Delap, Carol
Goldenwest High School, Visalia

Estes, Marianne
La Mirada High School, La Mirada

Ford, Pam
Temecula Valley High School, Temecula

Geer, Donna, Assistant Principal
Chino High School, Chino

Glennan, Renee
Sequoia Jr. High School, Simi Valley

Grohmann, Joyce
Bellflower High School, Bellflower

Henderson, Gerry
Temple City High School, Temple City

Hibma, Grace
Office of Los Angeles County
Superintendent of Schools, Consultant,
Consumer & Homemaking Education

Himenes, Peggy
Actis Jr. High School, Bakersfield

Hulen, Donna Lyn
Los Alamitos High School,
Los Alamitos

Jones, Dotti
Etiwanda High School, Etiwanda

Lash, Mary
Paramount High School, Paramount

Lundy, Jeri
Grossmont High School, La Mesa

Lopez, Karen
San Luis Obispo High School
San Luis Obispo

Matsuno, Dale
Bell Gardens High School,
Bell Gardens

Pendleton, Susie
Cerritos High School, Cerritos

Phipps, Louise
Washington Middle School, Vista

Pereira, Marilyn
Hanford High School, Hanford

Priestley, Roberta
Alhambra High School,
Alhambra

Pringle, Adrienne
Royal High School, Simi Valley

Richmond, Mary E.
San Luis Obispo High School,
San Luis Obispo

Ruth, Lynda
La Mirada High School, La Mirada

Sheats, Dianne
Gridley High School, Gridley

Shepherd, Maxine
Moreno Valley High School,
Moreno Valley

Shrock, Bonnie
Kearny High School, San Diego

Titus, Karen
Fullerton College, Fullerton

Traw, Marianne
Ball Jr. High School, Anaheim

Wells, Betty
Oroville High School, Oroville

Wetzel, Naomi, retired
Delta High School, Clarksburg

Whitten, Kathryn P.
Regional Supervisor Home
Economics Education, Fresno

Wildermuth, Ellie
La Canada High School, La Canada

HALLOWEEN

WITCHES BREW

Serves 20

2 quarts apple cider, chilled
1 (6 ounce) frozen grape juice
  concentrate, thawed

1 pint orange sherbet
1 (33.8 ounce) bottle ginger ale, chilled

Combine apple cider and grape juice concentrate in a 5 to 6 quart punch bowl. Scoop out orange sherbet and float on top of punch. Add ginger ale. Stir gently to combine ingredients and make top look frothy.

"Devilishly good punch for children's party."

Cathy Miller   **Montclair High School, Montclair, CA**

HOT SPICED CIDER

Serves 16

2 quarts apple cider
1/2 cup brown sugar
1/2 teaspoon whole allspice
1 cinnamon stick

dash nutmeg
1/4 teaspoon salt
1 orange (unpeeled, cut into wedges)

Pour cider in lower part of electric coffee maker. Place filter lined basket in coffee maker and put all remaining ingredients in basket. Cover and perk.

"I always make this for my faculty Christmas party; it goes before the coffee. However, it is a hit for any special occasion."

Roberta Priestley   **Alhambra High School, Alhambra, CA**

HOMEMADE ROOT BEER

Serves a lot

1 gallon water
1 pound granulated sugar

2 teaspoons root beer concentrate
1 pound dry ice

Pour water into a large container. Add sugar and root beer concentrate. Stir. Add dry ice. Let set about 30 minutes.

"This is really fun for a Halloween party because it resembles a steaming cauldron."

Jan Oliver   **Irvine High School, Irvine, CA**

CREEPY CHEESE PUFFS

Makes 30 to 40 pieces

1 box phyllo (filo) dough
2 cups cheese, grated (sharp yellow
  is best)

herb of your choice (I prefer dill)
1/2 cup butter, melted

Lay filo dough on counter (2 to 3 sheets). Sprinkle with cheese (about ½ cup) and a small amount of herb. Roll on a ½" dowel. Push together while still on dowel, until about 8 inches long. Remove dowel, brush with melted butter. Cut into 1 inch pieces. Place on a pammed (spray with cooking spray) cookie sheet cut side up. Bake at 425 degrees for 5 to 10 minutes. (May be made ahead of time and baked right before serving.)

"A favorite with clients when I was in the catering business."

Susie Pendleton   **Cerritos High School, Cerritos, CA**

CARAMEL APPLES

Serves 6

6 apples	*1 (14 ounce) can sweetened*
6 wooden skewers	*condensed milk*
butter or margarine for coating	*⅛ teaspoon salt*
1 cup sugar	*¼ cup butter or margarine*
¾ cup white corn syrup	*1 teaspoon vanilla*

Wash and thoroughly dry each apple. Remove stems. Insert skewer into stem end of each and set aside in refrigerator. Coat waxed paper with butter or margarine and place on a tray. In a heavy saucepan, combine sugar, corn syrup, sweetened condensed milk and salt; mix well. Cook over medium heat, stirring gently but constantly until it reaches 230 degrees on a candy thermometer or until a small amount dropped in cold water forms a soft ball (about 30 minutes). Remove from heat and cool slightly. Stir in ¼ cup butter or margarine and vanilla. Working quickly, dip apples in caramel to coat well. Place stem side up on waxed paper to harden. Cool in refrigerator.

"This recipe also makes a great ice cream topping. You can also harden the caramel in a greased bread pan, cut into squares and wrap separately for candy."

Peg Della Zoppa   **Yucca Valley High School, Yucca Valley, CA**

CARAMEL CORN

Makes 5 quarts

5 quarts popped corn	*½ cup light corn syrup*
2 cubes butter	*1 teaspoon vanilla*
1 pound brown sugar	*1 teaspoon baking soda*
1 teaspoon cream of tartar	*1 can Spanish peanuts, optional*

In a saucepan, combine butter, sugar, cream of tartar and corn syrup; boil 3 minutes. Stir in vanilla and baking soda; mixture will "bubble up." Put popcorn in a large pan, sprinkle with Spanish peanuts, and pour mixture over popcorn, stirring to coat and mix in peanuts. Bake at 250 degrees in oven for 1 hour, stirring every 15 minutes.

"I use a large turkey aluminum roasting pan -- the throw away kind!"

Kathleen Daudistel   **Hanford High School, Hanford, CA**

CARAMEL POPCORN BALLS

Makes 16

8 cups popped corn
¾ cup sugar
¾ cup brown sugar
½ cup light corn syrup

½ cup water
1 teaspoon white vinegar
¼ teaspoon salt
¾ cup butter or margarine

Measure popped corn into a large bowl. Combine sugars, corn syrup, water, vinegar, and salt in a 2 quart saucepan. Heat pan to boiling over medium heat, stirring frequently. Cook, stirring constantly until mixture dropped into very cold water forms a hard ball (or 260 degrees on a candy thermometer). Reduce heat to low; stir in butter or margarine until melted. Pour syrup in thin stream over popped corn in bowl, stirring until popcorn is well coated. Cool slightly. Butter hands; generously shape into 3 inch balls and place on waxed paper. Wrap in plastic wrap when cooled.

"A real family tradition and fun for Halloween. You can also decorate these and make pumpkin faces if you like."

Beverly Ranger   Carpenteria High School, Carpenteria, CA

CHOCOLATE POPCORN BALLS

Makes about 1½ dozen   **Photo on Page 61**

1 (3.5 oz.) bag microwave popping
    corn, popped or 10 cups
    popped popcorn
½ cup light brown sugar, packed

¼ cup light corn syrup
1½ squares (1½ oz.) HERSHEY'S
    Unsweetened Baking Chocolate
2 tablespoons butter or margarine

Butter large bowl; cover tray with wax paper. Prepare popcorn according to manufacturer's instructions; place in prepared bowl, discarding any unpopped kernels. In small saucepan, stir together brown sugar, corn syrup, chocolate and butter. Cook over medium heat, stirring constantly, until mixture comes to full rolling boil; continue boiling and stirring 1 minute. Remove from heat; immediately pour chocolate mixture over popcorn. Stir until popcorn is evenly coated. With buttered hands, shape into 2-inch diameter balls; place on prepared tray. Cool completely; place in paper muffin cups (2½ inches in diameter), if desired. Store in airtight container in cool, dry place.

Hershey Foods Corporation, Hershey, PA

HONEYED POPCORN BALLS

Makes 12 2" popcorn balls

1½ quarts popped corn
½ cup brown sugar, firmly packed
½ cup sugar

¼ cup honey or corn syrup
⅓ cup water
1 tablespoon butter

Put popped corn in a large bowl or metal dishpan; place in warm oven (250 degrees). Combine sugars, honey and water in a 2-quart saucepan. Heat slowly, stirring until sugar is dissolved. Cook to firm ball stage (242 degrees). Add butter and stir only enough to mix. Slowly pour the hot syrup over warm popped corn, mix thoroughly. With buttered palms and fingers, shape immediately into balls slightly larger than a baseball, using as little pressure as possible.

Maxine Shepherd   **Moreno Valley High School, Moreno Valley, CA**

PUMPKIN-EATER DONUTS

Makes 2 dozen

2 tablespoons shortening
3/4 cup sugar
2 eggs
1 cup canned pumpkin
1 cup shredded bran cereal
2 3/4 cups flour

2 teaspoons baking powder
1 teaspoon pumpkin pie spice
1/2 teaspoon salt
vegetable oil for frying
1 cup cinnamon-sugar

Beat shortening and sugar in a large bowl until fluffy. Beat in eggs, one at a time. Stir in pumpkin, then cereal. Let stand 2 minutes. Sift flour, baking powder, spice and salt together; stir into pumpkin mixture, half at a time. Cover and chill one hour or until dough is stiff enough to handle. Roll out on a lightly floured board to 1/2 inch thick. Cut into rounds with hole in center. In a large pan, heat 2 inches of oil and fry until golden brown (about 2 minutes) on each side. Drain and dip in cinnamon-sugar if desired.

"This is wonderful for Halloween parties and surprise -- it's nutritious!"

Loretta Salau   **Foothill High School, Bakersfield, CA**

HALLOWEEN COOKIES

Makes 4 dozen

2 cups sugar
1 1/2 cups shortening
2 eggs
1/2 cup molasses
4 cups flour
2 teaspoons cloves
4 teaspoons baking soda
2 teaspoons cinnamon

2 teaspoons ginger
1 teaspoon salt
Decorator Icing
1 (pound) box powdered sugar
3/4 cup shortening or margarine
1/4 cup milk
1 teaspoon vanilla flavoring
small amount of orange paste coloring

Cream sugar and shortening. Add the eggs and beat well. Mix in the remaining ingredients. Roll the dough into small balls (the size of walnuts). Roll each cookie in granulated sugar. Place the cookies two inches apart on a greased cookie sheet. Press each cookie ¼ inch thick (use a glass). Bake at 350 degrees for 6 to 8 minutes. (Do not overbake). Cool. Decorate each cookie with orange tinted icing, raisins and candy corn.

For Icing: Beat all the ingredients 10 minutes with an electric mixer.

Bonnie Landin　　　　　**Garden Grove High School, Garden Grove, CA**

PUMPKIN COOKIES

Makes 4 dozen

1 cup vegetable shortening　　　*1 teaspoon baking powder*
1 cup sugar　　　*½ teaspoon baking soda*
1 cup pumpkin　　　*1 teaspoon ground cinnamon*
1 egg　　　*½ teaspoon ground nutmeg*
1 teaspoon vanilla　　　*½ teaspoon ground allspice*
2 cups flour　　　*½ cup nuts, chopped*
½ teaspoon salt

Preheat oven to 350 degrees. Cream the shortening and sugar well. Add pumpkin, egg, vanilla; mix well. Stir in remaining ingredients. Drop rounded teaspoonfuls 2 inches apart on a greased cookie sheet. Sprinkle with a mixture of cinnamon and sugar, if desired. Bake for 12 to 15 minutes. Cool on wire rack; store in covered container to keep soft.

Rita Blohm　　　　　**Nogales High School, La Puente, CA**

CHOCOLATE CHIP PUMPKIN COOKIES

Makes 4 to 5 dozen

1 cup liquid shortening　　　*2 teaspoons nutmeg*
3 cups sugar　　　*2 teaspoons cinnamon*
2 eggs　　　*1 large can pumpkin*
5 cups sifted flour　　　*2 cups chocolate chip*
2 teaspoons baking powder　　　*1 cup nuts, chopped*
2 teaspoons baking soda　　　*2 teaspoons vanilla*
1 teaspoon salt

Mix shortening and sugar; add eggs and beat well. Sift together flour, baking powder, baking soda, salt and spices. Mix flour mixture alternately with pumpkin then shortening and sugar mixture. Beat after each addition. Fold in chocolate chips, nuts, and vanilla. Drop onto a greased cookie sheet and bake at 375 degrees for 10 minutes.

"Very moist!"

Pamela Fecchino　　　　　**Cimarron-Memorial High School, Las Vegas, NV**

HARVEST PUMPKIN BARS

Makes 24 bars

2 cups flour
2 teaspoons baking powder
1½ teaspoons cinnamon
½ teaspoon nutmeg
4 eggs
1 (16 ounce) can pumpkin
1⅔ cups sugar

1 cup oil
1 cup walnuts, chopped
3 ounces cream cheese
¼ cup margarine
1 teaspoon vanilla
2 cups powdered sugar

Combine flour, baking powder, cinnamon and nutmeg in a large bowl. Set aside. In a medium bowl, beat eggs, pumpkin, sugar and oil together. Add to first mixture. Stir in chopped walnuts (optional). Spread mixture into a greased and floured 13" x 9" pan. Bake at 350 degrees for 25 to 30 minutes, or until a toothpick inserted in center comes out clean. Cool before frosting.

To make frosting: Beat softened cream cheese, margarine and vanilla together in a small bowl. Slowly add sifted powdered sugar. Frost cooled pumpkin bars and cut into squares.

Sheryl Malone   **Mt. Carmel High School, San Diego, CA**

PUMPKIN BREAD

Makes 2 standard loaves or 7 miniature loaves

4 eggs
3 cups sugar
1 cup oil
3 cups flour
2 teaspoons baking soda
½ teaspoon baking powder
2 teaspoons cinnamon

1 teaspoon nutmeg
1 teaspoon cloves
1 teaspoon allspice
¾ teaspoon salt
2 cups pumpkin
⅔ cups water

Beat eggs, sugar and oil. Sift dry ingredients together and add to egg, sugar and oil mixture. Add pumpkin and water. Pour into oiled and floured pans. Bake at 350 degrees, 1 hour, 15 minutes for 2 standard loaves, 45 minutes for 7 miniature loaves.

"This recipe came from Dorothy Mootz, a teacher colleague. It is fabulous -- everyone likes it -- it is easy to make and freezes beautifully. A real winner!"

Phyllis Kaylor   **Ray Kroc Middle School, San Diego, CA**

PUMPKIN MUFFINS

Serves 12

1 cup sugar
½ cup oil
1 cup cooked pumpkin
½ cup water
2 eggs
1½ cups flour

¼ teaspoon salt
1½ teaspoon baking soda
½ teaspoon nutmeg
½ teaspoon cinnamon
⅔ cups nuts, chopped

Mix first five ingredients until well blended. Add the other ingredients and mix. Lightly grease and flour a muffin tin or use paper liners. Fill the muffin cups and bake at 350 degrees for 25 to 30 minutes.

"Use your Halloween pumpkin! Steam it, blend it and then follow the recipe. These muffins are easy enough for students to try and make."

Diana Hill   **Sunnymead Middle School, Moreno Valley, CA**

APPLE STREUSEL MUFFINS

Makes 18

2 cups flour, sifted
1 cup sugar (can be reduced to
    ¾ cup)
1 tablespoon baking powder
1¼ teaspoons cinnamon
½ teaspoon baking soda
2 large eggs
1 cup sour cream

¼ cup butter or margarine, melted
1 cup apple, finely diced
    (peeled or unpeeled)
Topping:
¼ cup sugar
3 tablespoons flour
¼ teaspoon cinnamon
2 tablespoons butter, cut in

Sift and combine all dry ingredients for the muffins. Combine eggs, sour cream and butter and add to the dry ingredients. Add the finely diced apple and stir just enough to combine all ingredients. In a separate bowl, combine the topping ingredients, cutting butter in and mix until crumbly. Spoon muffin mixture into muffin papers, filling about ¾ full. Sprinkle topping mixture on top. Bake at 400 degrees for approximately 20 to 25 minutes. Check at 20 minutes and watch carefully so as not to overcook.

"This is a recipe from a friend of mine in Iowa. She always bakes the most delicious things and this is one of her personal favorites."

Patti Ligon   **Granite Hills High School, El Cajon, CA**

HALLOWEEN CREAM OF PUMPKIN SOUP

Serves 6

3 pounds pumpkin
1 large onion, chopped
2 tablespoons butter or margarine
2½ cups water

salt and pepper to taste
3 eggs, beaten
2½ cups milk
grated cheese

Cook the pumpkin until tender and puree in a blender. Saute the onion in butter or margarine until transparent. Put onion into a saucepan with the pumpkin, water, salt and pepper and simmer for about 1 hour. Mix eggs with milk and add to the soup. Heat the soup gently for a few minutes to cook the eggs, taking care not to boil or the eggs will curdle. Garnish with grated cheese.

"This is a simple soup to make ahead to serve on Halloween when there are a lot of ghosts and goblins at your door."

Jeri Drake Lane   Canyon Springs High School, Moreno Valley, CA

MANDARIN CARROTS

Serves 4 to 6

4 cups carrots
2 tablespoons butter
1 (11 oz.) can mandarin oranges

¼ cup brown sugar
½ teaspoon salt
¼ teaspoon ground ginger

Cut carrots in 2 inch pieces. Put carrots and butter in a 1½ quart glass casserole. Cook on high in microwave for 10 minutes, covered. Turn dish once during cook time. Add oranges, sugar, salt and ginger. Cook three more minutes. Stand for 4 to 5 minutes before serving.

"We run out of burners on busy holidays, using the microwave for the vegetable helps.

Lynda Ruth   La Mirada High School, La Mirada, CA

HALLOWEEN CHICKEN PIZZA MASKS

Makes 12 mini-pizzas   **Photo on Page 28**

1 pound ground chicken
⅓ cup onion, chopped
1 teaspoon salt
½ teaspoon pepper
1 package (6 count) English
   muffins, split
2 tablespoons soft margarine, divided

1½ cups bottled pizza sauce, divided
1 teaspoon oregano
1 large green pepper
4 ounces Cheddar cheese, shredded
4 ounces mozzarella cheese, shredded
3 large pitted ripe olives, each sliced
   into 4 rings

Heat frypan to medium-high temperature. Add ground chicken and onion. Season with salt and pepper; cook, stirring, until all red is gone, about 6 minutes. Set aside. With aluminum foil, cover 10½ by 15½-inch baking pan. Spread each muffin half with ½ teaspoon margarine and arrange in single layer on prepared pan. Spread heaping tablespoon pizza sauce on each muffin half. Cover generously with ground chicken and onion; sprinkle with oregano. Cut 12 slivers of green pepper into "smiling" mouth shapes and set aside; chop remaining pepper and sprinkle on pizzas. Mix together Cheddar and mozzarella cheese; sprinkle generously on mini-pizzas. Place in 450 degree oven about 12 minutes. Remove from oven. Make mask face on each pizza by using 2 ripe olive rings for eyes and pepper slice for mouth. Turn some slices up for smiles and some down for frowns.

"Per Serving: Calories: 244, Protein: 16.4 grams, Total Fat: 11.0 grams, Saturated Fat: 4.95 grams, Carbohydrates: 19.5 grams, Cholesterol: 56 milligrams, Sodium: 567 milligrams."

National Broiler Council   **Washington, D.C.**

VEGETARIAN CHILI

Serves 8 to 10

1 tablespoon oil	*2 teaspoons chili powder*
1 cup celery, chopped (leaves too)	*½ teaspoon salt*
1 cup onion, chopped	*cayenne pepper to taste*
½ teaspoon garlic salt	*1 (15 ounce) can tomato sauce*
½ teaspoon celery salt	*2 (1 pound 1 ounce) can kidney or*
1 (1 pound 12 ounce) can tomatoes	*chili beans, undrained*

In the oil, saute celery and onion until tender. Add the rest of the ingredients in the order given. Simmer for 2 hours. If it needs to be thicker, thicken with 1 to 2 tablespoons cornstarch.

Note: Can also add ½ cup green pepper, chopped, while sauteing onions and celery.

"This can easily be converted to "meat" chili by adding 1 to 2 pounds ground meat first!"

Carolyn Cummings   **Newhart Middle School, Mission Viejo, CA**

SAUSAGE STEW

Serves 8

2 pounds sausage (we like Italian)	*½ cup bell pepper*
1½ cups mushrooms, quartered	*½ to 1 cup onion*
1½ cups zucchini	*2 cans stewed tomatoes*

Cut sausages into 1 inch, bite-sized pieces. Brown. Chop all vegetables into bite-sized pieces. Place all ingredients in a large pot. Cover with water. Simmer 20 minutes to 1 hour at medium high heat.

"As you can see by the ingredients, you may add or subtract as your tastebuds prefer. This recipe became a favorite when Brian married my daughter, Gail, and became our 'son-in-love'."

Sue Walters   **Morse High School, San Diego, CA**

THANKSGIVING

CRANBERRY PEAR RELISH

Serves 18

12 ounces fresh or frozen cranberries
1 large pear, halved and cored
   (8 to 9 ounces)

1 small Valencia orange (5 ounces)
¼ cup walnuts
½ cup sugar

Rinse and drain cranberries. Coarsely chop cranberries, pear, orange (remove seeds, but leave rind on) and walnuts. Mix together all ingredients and store in a plastic container in the refrigerator. This can be made 2 to 3 days in advance.

"There are only 52 calories in a serving."

Nancy Bohte   **South Pasadena High School, So. Pasadena, CA**

CINNAMON APPLES

Serves 8 to 10

10 to 12 apples, washed, peeled, cored
   and quartered
1 cup Karo syrup

⅓ cup sugar
1 bag cinnamon candies ("Red Hots")

Place prepared apples in a large saucepan. Add Karo syrup and sugar. Bring to a boil over medium heat. Add cinnamon candy. Reduce heat to simmer. Cook for 15 to 20 minutes or until apples are tender and a bright red color. Serve warm or cold in a clear glass bowl.

"A colorful accompaniment for turkey or ham."

Sally Oxford   **Monache High School, Porterville, CA**

CAPE COD CRANBERRY NUT BREAD

Makes 1 loaf

2 cups flour, sifted
1½ teaspoons baking powder
½ teaspoon soda
1 egg
1 cup sugar

2 tablespoons margarine
½ cup orange juice plus ¼ cup water
1 cup raw cranberries, cut in halves
½ cup walnuts, chopped

Sift together flour, baking powder and soda. Mix together egg, sugar, and margarine. Add dry ingredients alternately with orange juice mixture. Blend in cranberries and walnuts. Pour into greased loaf pan and bake for 1 hour at 350 degrees.

Carolyn McBride   **Arcadia High School, Arcadia, CA**

NUT LOAF

Serves 9

3 eggs, lightly beaten
¾ cup lowfat milk
3 cups nuts, finely grated
*   (I prefer almonds)*
1 onion, finely chopped
3 cloves garlic, finely chopped
5 ribs celery, finely chopped
1 cup wheat germ

1½ cup cooked brown rice OR
*   raw rolled oats*
2 tablespoons soy sauce
½ teaspoon rosemary
½ teaspoon sage
1 teaspoon caraway seeds
salt to taste

Mix all ingredients together in a large bowl until well blended. Turn into an oiled 9" x 5" x 3" loaf pan and bake 50 to 60 minutes at 350 degrees. Serve like a meat loaf. The nut loaf, when cold, can be spread on crackers with cream cheese.

"I developed this recipe for my vegetarian husband -- to eat in lieu of turkey. But now, he has to fight off the kids! It is everyone's favorite Thanksgiving food."

Phyllis Kaylor   **Ray Kroc Middle School, San Diego, CA**

PERSIMMON BREAD

Makes 1 loaf

2 teaspoons baking soda
2 cups persimmon pulp
2 cups sugar
1 cup margarine
2 eggs
2 cups flour

1 teaspoon cinnamon
1 teaspoon salt
1 teaspoon cloves
1 teaspoon nutmeg or allspice
1 cup nuts
1 cup raisins (optional)

Dissolve baking soda in persimmon pulp. Combine sugar and margarine. Cream together. Add pulp and soda mixture and blend. Add eggs and mix. Add together in a separate bowl, the flour, cinnamon, salt, cloves and nutmeg. Add to the other mixture and stir. Fold in nuts and raisins. Pour into greased and floured 9" x 5" loaf pan. It's best to line the bottom of the pan with waxed paper. Bake at 300 degrees for 30 minutes, then reduce heat to 250 degrees and bake an additional 30 to 45 minutes. For extra moist bread, put a small pan of water in the bottom of oven.

"A great Christmas treat to give as gifts."

RoseMary Ross   **North High School, Bakersfield, CA**

NO FUSS PUMPKIN BREAD

Makes 2 loaves

3½ cups sugar
3½ cups flour
2 teaspoons baking soda
1 teaspoon nutmeg
1 teaspoon cinnamon
1 teaspoon allspice

4 eggs
1 cup oil
1 teaspoon vanilla
1 cup nuts, chopped
2 cups mashed pumpkin

Preheat oven to 350 degrees. Sift all dry ingredients together. Add eggs, oil, vanilla and pumpkin; beat until smooth. Stir in chopped nuts. Bake in two, greased and floured, loaf pans for 40 to 45 minutes or until done.

Delores Singleton   **Cheyenne High School, Las Vegas, NV**

ORANGE SPICE MUFFINS

Makes 2 dozen

2 eggs
2 cups buttermilk
½ cup oil
⅞ cup honey
3 cups bran
2 cups flour

½ cup whole wheat flour
1 tablespoon baking soda
½ teaspoon salt
Cloves, nutmeg, and cinnamon to taste
2 orange peels

Mix eggs, buttermilk, oil and honey. In a separate bowl, mix bran, flours, baking soda, salt, cloves, nutmeg, cinnamon and orange peels. Combine wet and dry ingredients and spoon into oiled muffin tins. Bake at 400 degrees for 15 to 20 minutes.

Joy Sweeney-Aiello   **Liberty High School, Brentwood, CA**

RAISIN BRAN MUFFINS

Makes a lot

1 (15 ounce) box raisin bran
  flake cereal
5 cups flour
5 teaspoons baking soda
2 teaspoons salt

3 cups sugar
1 quart buttermilk
1 cup oil
4 eggs, well beaten

Mix dry ingredients together. Add liquid ingredients and stir until moistened. Fill muffin tins two thirds full, and bake at 400 degrees for 18 to 20 minutes.

"Dough may be stored up to 6 weeks."

Barbara Bressler   **Buena Park High School, Buena Park, CA**

CREAM OF TURKEY SOUP

Serves 4

½ cup onion, diced
½ cup carrots, diced
½ cup celery, diced
1 clove garlic, minced
5 tablespoons turkey fat or margarine
5 tablespoons flour

2 cups turkey or chicken broth
Salt and white pepper to taste
Sweet basil to taste
3 cups hot milk or half & half
1 to 2 cups turkey, cooked and diced

Saute all vegetables and garlic in fat or margarine until they are tender. Add flour to make a roux; add chicken or turkey broth. Cook and stir to make a very thick soup. Season to taste with salt, white pepper and sweet basil. Stir in milk or half & half and turkey. Cook below boiling for about 5 minutes more. Garnish before serving with chopped green onion, parsley or pimento.

"This recipe came from Mr. Perry's Family Restaurant in Sacramento and is a tasty and easy way to use up leftover turkey."

Kay Linberger   **Tokay High School, Lodi, CA**

CARROT SALAD

Serves 10-12

2 pounds carrots
1 can tomato soup
2 cups onions, chopped
2 cups green pepper, chopped
1 cup sugar

¾ cup white vinegar
⅓ cup vegetable oil
1 teaspoon mustard
1 teaspoon worcestershire sauce

Slice and cook carrots in salted water until tender. Drain. Marinate in: soup, onion, green pepper, sugar, vinegar, oil, mustard and worcestershire sauce. Cover and refrigerate 2 to 3 days ahead of using.

"This salad adds variety to a formal meal or is great for a pot luck. It's surprisingly delicious, cold and colorful."

Jan Oliver   **Irvine High School, Irvine, CA**

FRESH CRANBERRY SALAD

Serves 6-8

1 red apple, unpeeled
1 green apple, unpeeled
1 pear, peeled
1 orange, peeled

2 cups fresh cranberries
½ cup sugar (approximate)
1 tablespoon cinnamon
1 cup walnuts or pecans, chopped

Core and remove seeds from apples, pear, and orange. Using a food processor chop all fruit. Gently toss in a large bowl adding sugar, cinnamon and nuts.

"This is great served as an accompaniment salad, as a fruit 'relish' with tortilla chips or add to jello for a wonderful molded salad."

Colleen Easton   **Brea Olinda High School, Brea, CA**

KIWI FRUIT SALAD

Serves 6

1 medium-sized pineapple, cut into
*   1 inch cubes*
3 bananas, sliced diagonally
2 firm, ripe Japanese-style
persimmons, cut into thin slices
1 cup red grapes
6 kiwi fruit, peeled and sliced
walnuts or pecans, chopped

Honey Yogurt Dressing:
1½ tablespoons grated orange peel
1 teaspoon grated fresh ginger
¾ cup mayonnaise
¾ cup plain yogurt
2 tablespoons honey
1 tablespoon lemon juice

In a large bowl, gently mix together the fruit. Chill for 30 minutes before serving. Add nuts just before serving. Blend together dressing ingredients with a wire whisk. Pass dressing to spoon over individual servings.

Anna Atkin   **Monache High School, Porterville, CA**

WINTER FRUIT SALAD

Serves 10 to 12

3 cans grapefruit, drained
2 cans mandarin oranges, drained
1 can pineapple tidbits, drained
2 cans tropical fruit

red grapes, cut in half
4 apples, chopped into pieces
2 bananas, sliced
½ bag miniature marshmallows

Mix all of the above ingredients with the juice from the tropical fruit. Serve immediately.

"This fruit salad is great with Thanksgiving dinner. It can be made the night before, but add the marshmallows right before serving."

Marla Maiorano   **Mt. Carmel High School, San Diego, CA**

ALMOND ORANGE SALAD

Serves 6 to 8

Dressing:
$^1\!/_2$ cup salad oil
4 tablespoons sugar
4 tablespoons vinegar
1 teaspoon salt
$^1\!/_4$ teaspoon white pepper
tabasco sauce
1 tablespoon sugar

$^1\!/_4$ cup sliced almonds
1 head romaine lettuce
1 cup celery, chopped
3 green onions, chopped
1 tablespoon parsley, chopped
1 (11 ounce) can mandarin oranges,
    drained
sugar coated almonds for garnish

Mix all dressing ingredients and refrigerate overnight. Melt 1 tablespoon sugar in a skillet over low heat until dissolved. Add almonds, stirring until sugar coated. Set aside. Toss salad mixings with salad dressing. Sprinkle sugar coated almonds on top and serve.

"I like this with turkey at Thanksgiving -- the oranges in this salad are good flavor accompaniment with usual cranberries and dressing. My daughter likes this salad...the best compliment it could receive. It is a special recipe from Magic Keys to Cooking Cookbook."

Luann Goedert   **Carlsbad High School, Carlsbad, CA**

SPECTACULAR HOT FRUIT SALAD

Serves 8 to 10

$2^1\!/_2$ cups assorted fruits, cut up and
    drained (fresh fruit or canned, such
    as pears, peaches and pineapple)
$^1\!/_2$ cup maraschino cherries, drained
2 bananas, sliced about $^1\!/_4$" thick

1 cup black cherries, pitted and
    drained
$^1\!/_2$ cup brown sugar
2 tablespoons cornstarch
1 tablespoon curry powder
$^1\!/_2$ cup butter or margarine, melted

Preheat oven to 350 degrees. Combine first four ingredients in a casserole dish. In a bowl, mix together the brown sugar, cornstarch and curry. Add melted butter or margarine to the fruit; then add sugar mixture to fruit. Stir lightly. Bake at 350 degrees for 40 minutes.

Note: It is best enjoyed when served in small amounts, as in a custard cup.

"This hot fruit salad is almost a "one of a kind" since it is so unusual. My grandmother prepared it for holiday feasts to accompany turkey or ham."

Vicki Agee   **San Marcos High School, San Marcos, CA**

FESTIVE SALAD

Serves 10 to 12

1 (6 ounce) package raspberry gelatin
1 (20 ounce) can crushed pineapple,
drained

1 can whole cranberries

Make gelatin according to package directions being sure to decrease water if you're making a molded salad. You might want to substitute the drained juice for some of the water. Mix in pineapple and cranberries. Chill until set.

Mary Cronkhite　　　　**Antelope Valley High School, Lancaster, CA**

BISHOP'S STUFFING

Serves 12 or more

1 box cornbread mix
8 hamburger buns
1 pound ground sausage
1½ pounds ground beef
1 large rib celery, chopped
3 large onions, chopped

1 to 2 apples, chopped (optional)
1 to 2 cubes butter, melted
3 cans chopped black olives
2 cups pecans, coarsely chopped
salt and pepper to taste
poultry seasoning to taste

Prepare cornbread mix according to box instructions; bake and cool. Crumble cornbread and hamburger buns together. Brown sausage, ground beef, celery, onions and apples together. Add some water; bring to a boil and then simmer, letting the mixture steam down. In a very large container, mix together the bread mixture, meat mixture, melted butter, olives, pecans, salt, pepper and poultry seasoning to taste. Stuff in turkey or chicken or heat in a casserole dish for 45 minutes at 350 degrees.

"This stuffing can be made a few weeks ahead and frozen. It's wonderful stuffed in a turkey or chicken or heated in casserole and used as a side dish to round out any meal."

Marilyn Bankhead　　　　**San Marcos High School, San Marcos, CA**

"GRANDMA'S" CORN BREAD DRESSING

Serves 6 to 8

1 cup celery and leaves, diced
1 large onion, diced
butter
2 cups corn bread crumbs

2 cups dry bread or biscuit crumbs
salt and pepper to taste
poultry seasoning to taste
stock

Saute celery and onion in butter until tender (not brown). Mix with crumbs. Season to taste with salt, pepper and poultry seasoning. Moisten with stock from giblets which have been boiled until tender. Dressing should be moist enough to toss lightly.

GRANDPA'S TURKEY STUFFING

Stuffs one turkey

¼ onion, finely chopped
1 tablespoon butter
½ cup water
1 cube chicken bouillon
1 pound ground beef

1 egg
1 teaspoon poultry seasoning
salt and pepper to taste
1 (8 ounce) package bread stuffing

Saute onions in butter until tender. Boil water and add bouillon cube; stir until dissolved. Place ground beef in a large bowl. Add egg, poultry seasoning, salt and pepper. Mix together. Place bread stuffing in another bowl; add bouillon and blend until moistened. Add onions to meat mixture, blend, then add bread stuffing and mix like a meat loaf. Brown the stuffing mixture in a large skillet until completely cooked before stuffing into the turkey.

"As the name implies -- this is my grandpa's recipe, and it wouldn't be Thanksgiving without it...in fact, the recipe is tripled and there are never any leftovers!!"

Marion S. Anderson   **A. G. Currie Middle School, Tustin, CA**

CORNBREAD-RICE STUFFING

Makes 15 cups

<u>Turkey Stock</u>
Turkey neck and gizzard
1 celery stalk, cut into pieces
1 carrot, cut into large pieces
½ yellow onion, coarsely chopped
<u>Turkey Stuffing</u>
¼ cup brandy
1 quart cold water
¾ cup uncooked wild rice
¼ cup olive oil
2 cups celery, thinly sliced
1 large yellow onion, minced
4 cloves garlic, minced
3 cups mushrooms, sliced
¾ cup fresh parsley, finely chopped

2 tablespoons fresh basil
  (or 2 teaspoons dried)
1 tablespoon each fresh rosemary,
  tarragon, thyme and oregano
  (or 1 teaspoon dried), finely
  chopped
11 cups crumbled day-old cornbread
1 (8 oz.) can sliced water chestnuts,
  drained & rinsed
1 cup toasted pine nuts
¾ teaspoon salt
½ teaspoon freshly ground black
  pepper
1 tablespoon unsalted butter, melted

Prepare stock. While stock simmers, make stuffing. In small saucepan, heat brandy until warm; remove from heat. In 2 quart saucepan, bring water to boiling. Add rice; boil 40 to 45 minutes or until tender. Set aside. In large skillet, heat oil over medium heat; add celery, onion and garlic. Saute 10 minutes. Add mushrooms and herbs; mix well (if using dried herbs, chop them with the parsley to freshen flavor). Saute 5 minutes longer.

Transfer celery mixture to large bowl; add the ¼ cup turkey stock, rice, cornbread, water chestnuts, pine nuts, salt and pepper. With hands, toss gently to combine. (Mixture should only be very slightly moist.) Preheat oven to 325 degrees. Stuff turkey with mixture (do not pack). Place extra stuffing in a greased 9 inch baking dish and drizzle with melted butter; cover. Bake stuffing the last 45 minutes turkey is in oven. To cook stuffing separately...place in a greased 13 x 9 inch baking dish. Drizzle with 2 tablespoons melted butter. Cover with lid or aluminum foil and bake 45 minutes in 325 degree oven.

Kathie Baczynski   **Mt. Carmel High School, San Diego, CA**

CALIFORNIA TURKEY BREAST WITH SPINACH DRESSING

Makes 6-8 servings   **Photo on Page 29**

1 half California-grown turkey breast
4 tablespoons butter
1 teaspoon thyme
2 fresh garlic cloves, cut in half
1 cup each onion and celery, chopped
1 package (10 ounces) frozen, chopped
   spinach, thawed, drained

¾ cup broth or water
3 slices wheat bread, cubed
1 cup toasted walnut pieces or
   pine nuts
¼ teaspoon nutmeg
Salt and pepper

Rub turkey breast with 1 tablespoon butter, thyme and garlic. In remaining butter, cook onion and celery until soft. Mix with remaining ingredients to make dressing. Place dressing in greased baking pan; cover with turkey breast, skin side up. Bake 1½ hours at 350 degrees.

Calif. Poultry Industry Federation   **Modesto, CA**

ONE PAN TURKEY 'N STUFFING

Makes 6 servings

1 cup baking mix (such as Bisquick)
1¼ cups milk
3 eggs
1 teaspoon parsley flakes
1 teaspoon dried sage leaves or
   ¾ teaspoon ground sage
¾ teaspoon dried thyme leaves

½ teaspoon salt
½ teaspoon poultry seasoning
⅛ teaspoon pepper
2 cups cut-up cooked turkey
1 cup celery, chopped
½ cup onion, finely chopped

Heat oven to 400 degrees. Grease rectangular baking dish (10" x 6" x 1½"). Mix baking mix, milk, eggs, parsley, sage, thyme, salt, poultry seasoning and pepper in dish with fork until batter is of uniform color (batter will be lumpy). Stir in remaining ingredients. Bake until golden brown and knife inserted in center comes out clean. Bake for 35 to 40 minutes for a 10" dish; 30 to 35 minutes for an 11" dish.

"One pan just means it's easy. Just mix and bake in one pan."

Joyce Grohmann   **Bellflower High School, Bellflower, CA**

GREEN CHILE/TURKEY ENCHILADAS

Serves 10

3 cans cream of mushroom soup
8 fresh green chiles or
    1 large can diced green chiles
1 pint sour cream
leftover turkey, cooked and diced

oil
30 tortillas (corn or flour)
2 pounds cheddar or longhorn cheese,
    grated

Mix and heat the soup and chiles. Stir in sour cream and turkey. Bring a little bit of oil to simmer. Soak each tortilla in oil, drain. Spread a large spoonful of soup mixture on each tortilla. Roll up. Place in a baking dish. Grate cheese over top. Bake for 20 minutes at 350 degrees.

"You can alter this recipe in various ways: use cream of celery or chicken soup, eliminate the sour cream, eliminate the turkey...!

Cheryle Apple   **Rio Vista High School, Rio Vista, CA**

WILD RICE WITH MUSHROOMS AND ALMONDS

Serves 10 to 12

½ cup butter or margarine
1 cup wild rice, well rinsed and
    drained
½ cup slivered almonds
2 tablespoons onion, chives, scallions
    or green pepper, chopped

½ pound fresh mushrooms, trimmed
    and sliced
3 cups chicken broth

Over moderate heat, place the butter or margarine, rice, almonds, onion or alternative and mushrooms in a heavy skillet and cook 8 to 10 minutes, stirring almost constantly. Transfer to a 2 quart casserole and add the broth. Cover tightly and bake in a preheated 325 degree oven for 1½ to 2 hours.

Note: You may substitute brown rice for ½ of the wild rice.

Shirley Wilcox   **Burbank High School, Burbank**

MAKE AHEAD MASHED POTATOES

Serves 4 to 6

2 pounds red potatoes
½ cup milk

3 tablespoons butter
⅓ cup whipping cream

Peel, boil, drain and mash potatoes. Mash potatoes only -- no liquid. Heat ½ cup milk with the butter and whipping cream. Take out ¼ cup of this mixture and refrigerate. Mix remaining milk mixture with potatoes. Salt and pepper to taste. Put into 1½ quart greased casserole dish. Cover and refrigerate. Take potatoes out of refrigerator 2 hours before you plan to eat. Pour reserved ¼ cup milk mixture over top. Let sit. Bake for 25 minutes at 350 degrees.

"Make this the day before to cut down preparations on the day of the holiday."

Carole Call   **Costa Mesa High School, Costa Mesa, CA**

MASHED POTATO CASSEROLE

Serves 12 to 15

4½ to 5 pounds russet potatoes
*   (8 large)*
1 (8 ounce) package cream cheese,
*   at room temperature*

1 cup sour cream
2 teaspoons garlic salt
½ teaspoon pepper
¼ cup butter or margarine

Peel potatoes. In a 5 quart pan, bring water to a boil; add potatoes and cover. Boil until tender throughout when pierced (about 40 minutes). Drain, then mash well. In a small bowl of electric mixer, beat cream cheese and sour cream until smooth; gradually add to potatoes, beating until smoothly blended. Beat in garlic salt and pepper. Turn mixture into a buttered shallow 3 or 5 quart casserole dish. Dot with butter or margarine. Cover with lid or foil. At this point, you may refrigerate up to 3 days. Bring to room temperature before baking. Bake, covered, at 400 degrees for 50 to 60 minutes (until heated through).

"This is great to do ahead for Thanksgiving or Christmas dinner."

Vicki Pearl   **Giano Intermediate School, La Puente, CA**

SWEET POTATO CASSEROLE WITH PECAN TOPPING

Serves 6 to 8

3 pounds sweet potatoes
¾ cup orange juice
2 tablespoons butter, melted
2 tablespons sugar
1½ teaspoon ground cinnamon
½ teaspoon ground nutmeg

Topping:
½ cup flour
¼ cup plus 2 tablespoons brown sugar,
*   packed*
½ teaspoon cinnamon
¼ cup butter, at room temperature
½ cup pecans, chopped

Preheat oven to 350 degrees. Place the sweet potatoes in a baking pan and bake until tender, about 1 hour. Butter an 8" x 8" x 2" square glass baking pan. Scrape sweet potato pulp from skins into a large bowl. Using an electric mixer, mash the sweet potatoes. Add all of the ingredients except for topping ingredients. Beat until sweet potatoes are smooth. Spoon potatoes into baking dish. For topping: Combine flour, brown sugar, and cinnamon in a medium bowl. Add butter and cut in until mixture resembles coarse crumbs. Mix in chopped pecans. Sprinkle pecan topping over potatoes. Continue to bake at 350 degrees until sweet potatoes are hot and pecan topping is dry, about 30 minutes. Serve warm.

"A pleasant but elegant change from ordinary holiday sweet potatoes!"

Laurie Bleecker   **Chino High School, Chino, CA**

SWEET POTATO NESTS

Serves 4

1 (16 ounce) can sweet potatoes, well drained and mashed	1/8 teaspoon nutmeg
	dash of ground cloves
2 tablespoons brown sugar	dash of salt
1 tablespoon margarine, melted	1/3 to 1/2 cup nuts, finely chopped
1/4 teaspoon cinnamon	miniature marshmallows

Combine sweet potatoes, sugar, margarine, spices and salt; mix well. Divide mixture into four portions; shape into balls. Roll in nuts. Place on a cookie sheet; indent center with a spoon to form nests. Bake at 350 degrees for 10 minutes. Fill centers with marshmallows; continue baking for 5 minutes or until marshmallows are lightly browned.

"Fun for the whole family to make and eat!"

Betty Byrne   **Vaca Peña Middle School, Vacaville, CA**

CRANBERRY YAM BAKE

Serves 6 to 8

1 (40 ounce) can yams, drained	1 teaspoon cinnamon
1 cup whole fresh cranberries	1/4 cup margarine
Topping:	1/2 cup oatmeal
1/2 cup brown sugar	1/2 cup flour

Cut yams into small chunks and combine with cranberries. Combine topping ingredients with a pastry cutter until crumbly. Toss topping crumbs with yams and cranberries. Bake, uncovered, for 40 to 45 minutes in a greased casserole dish at 350 degrees.

"Be prepared to give out copies of this recipe -- a welcome change to traditional yams."

Susan Eckert   **Orr Middle School, Las Vegas, NV**

YAMS WITH FRESH ORANGE SAUCE

Serves 12

6 medium sized purple yams
1 cup orange juice
1 tablespoon cornstarch
3 tablespoons butter, melted
1/3 cup brown sugar, firmly packed
1/3 cup white sugar

rind of 1/2 orange, grated
2 tablespoons white corn syrup
1/2 cup walnuts, chopped
1 red apple, sliced
1 green apple, sliced

Boil yams until tender, then skin and slice. Combine the orange juice, cornstarch, butter, sugars, orange rind, and corn syrup in a saucepan and heat until thickened. Alternate yam slices, walnuts and apple slices in a greased baking dish. Pour sauce over everything and bake 45 minutes at 350 degrees.

"I never ate yams until I happened upon this recipe. I added the walnuts and apples to the recipe for extra color and flavor."

Janet Tingley   **Atascadero High School, Atascadero, CA**

SWEET ONION CASSEROLE

Serves 8

1/2 cup long grain rice, uncooked
7 to 8 cups sweet onions
    (brown are fine)
1/4 cup butter, melted

1 cup swiss cheese, grated
2/3 cup half & half
1 teaspoon salt

Cook rice in 2 cups boiling water for 5 minutes. Drain and set aside. Slice onions. Cook them in the butter in a skillet until limp. Combine all ingredients in a 2 quart, greased casserole. Mix well and bake at 350 degrees for 1 hour.

"This is my daughter, Joanie's, recipe. It has become a family favorite for fall and winter celebrations."

Myrna Swearingen   **Corona High School, Corona, CA**

SWISS GREEN BEANS

Serves 8

2 (9 oz.) packages frozen green beans,
    french style
1/4 cup butter or margarine
1 1/2 teaspoons minced onion
2 1/2 tablespoons flour
1/4 teaspoon dry mustard

1/2 teaspoon salt
pepper to taste
1 cup milk
3/8 pound swiss cheese, cubed
1/4 cup cashews, chopped

Cook green beans; drain. Melt butter in saucepan. Add onions, flour, mustard, salt and pepper. Gradually add milk; cook and stir until smooth and thick. Add cheese and stir until melted. Combine sauce and beans. Pour into greased 1½ quart casserole. Sprinkle with nuts. (This now can be refrigerated and baked the next day.) Bake 20 minutes or until hot at 350 degrees.

"Thanksgiving is very special to me. We always share it with my cousin, Betty, and family. When it is my turn to cook, I always make these beans."

Judy Betz   **Greenfield Junior High School, Bakersfield, CA**

HARVEST CABBAGE CASSEROLE

Serves 8 to 10

½ cup margarine or butter
2 tablespoons bacon drippings
1 medium head cabbage, core
*   removed, chopped coarsely*
¼ teaspoon dry minced garlic

1 teaspoon caraway seed
1 (10¾ ounce) can cream of
*   mushroom soup, undiluted*
salt and pepper to taste

Melt butter and bacon drippings in large skillet. Add cabbage and cook until tender/crisp (approximately 10 minutes). Add all seasonings. Stir in soup. Can be kept in low oven until dinner is served.

"I keep bacon drippings in an ice cube tray in the freezer for handy use!"

Jan Pierre   **Cabrillo High School, Lompoc, CA**

PUMPKIN CHEESECAKE WITH SOUR CREAM TOPPING

Serves 12

Crust:
¾ cup graham cracker crumbs
½ cup pecans, finely chopped
¼ cup light brown sugar, finely packed
¼ cup granulated sugar
½ stick (¼ cup) unsalted butter,
*   melted and cooled*
OR
36 ginger snaps (finely crushed)
5 tablespoons sugar
6 tablespoons margarine
Filling:
1½ cups solid pack pumpkin
3 large eggs
1½ teaspoons cinnamon

½ teaspoon freshly grated nutmeg
½ teaspoon ground ginger
½ teaspoon salt
½ cup light brown sugar, firmly packed
3 (8 oz.) packages cream cheese, cut
*   into bits and softened*
½ cup granulated sugar
2 tablespoons heavy cream
1 tablespoon cornstarch
1 teaspoon vanilla
Topping:
2 cups sour cream
2 tablespoons granulated sugar
16 pecan halves for garnish

Make the crust: In a bowl, combine the cracker crumbs and remaining ingredients. Press the mixture into the bottom and ½ inch up the sides of a buttered 9 inch springform pan. Chill the crust for 1 hour. Make the filling: In a bowl, whisk together the pumpkin, eggs, cinnamon, nutmeg, ginger, salt and brown sugar; set aside. In a large bowl with an electric mixer, cream together the cream cheese and granulated sugar; beat in cream, cornstarch, vanilla, and pumpkin mixture. Beat until filling is smooth.

Pour the filling into the crust and bake in the middle of a preheated 350 degree oven for 50 to 55 minutes, or until the center is just set. Remove from oven and let cool on a rack for 5 minutes.

Make the topping: In a bowl, whisk together the sour cream and sugar. Spread mixture over the top of the cheesecake and bake for 5 minutes more. Let the cheesecake cool in the pan on a rack, then chill overnight, covered.

When ready to serve, remove the side of the pan and garnish the top with pecan halves.

"A delicious make-ahead dessert for a large group. This is a great alternative to pumpkin pie at Thanksgiving!"

Sue Campbell   **Chico Junior High School, Chico, CA**

SOUR CREAM PUMPKIN PIE

Serves 8

½ cup half and half	*½ teaspoon ginger*
1 cup sour cream	*½ teaspoon allspice*
1 cup canned pumpkin	*½ teaspoon nutmeg*
1 teaspoon vanilla	*¼ teaspoon cloves*
1 cup brown sugar, packed	*½ teaspoon salt*
1 tablespoon flour	*2 eggs, slightly beaten*
¾ teaspoon cinnamon	*1 unbaked 9" pie shell*

Combine half and half, sour cream, pumpkin, vanilla, brown sugar, flour, spices, salt and mix well. Beat in eggs, then turn filling into pie shell. Bake at 400 degrees for 20 minutes, then reduce heat and continue baking at 350 degrees for 40 minutes. Cool.

"My family enjoys the extra spices in this pie -- it is very flavorful."

Pamela Ford   **Temecula Valley High School, Temecula**

MAPLE PUMPKIN PIE

Makes 1 pie Photo on Page 29

15-oz. pkg. Pillsbury All Ready Pie
Crust
1 teaspoon flour
Base
2 (3-oz.) pkg. cream cheese
2 tablespoons sugar
½ teaspoon vanilla
Filling
½ cup firmly packed brown sugar
½ teaspoon cinnamon
½ teaspoon nutmeg

1 teaspoon maple flavor
2 eggs, separated
¼ cup whipping cream
2 tablespoons margarine or butter,
melted
1 (16-oz.) can pumpkin
¼ teaspoon cream of tartar
Glaze
2 tablespoons maple syrup
Pecan halves

Prepare pie crust according to package directions for 2-crust pie. Heat oven to 375 degrees. In small bowl, combine base ingredients; beat at medium speed until smooth and well blended. Spread mixture in bottom of pie crust-lined pan. Bake at 375 degrees for 10 to 12 minutes or until center is set to a light touch. Cool base 5 minutes. Reduce oven temperature to 350 degrees.

Meanwhile, in large bowl, combine brown sugar, cinnamon, nutmeg, maple flavor and egg yolks; mix well. Add whipping cream, margarine and pumpkin; mix until thoroughly blended. Set aside.

In small bowl, beat egg whites with cream of tartar until stiff peaks form. Gently fold into pumpkin mixture; pour over cream cheese layer.

To make a lattice top, cut remaining crust into 12 strips about ¾ inch wide. Arrange strips in lattice design over pumpkin mixture. Seal and flute edges.

Bake at 350 degrees for 50 to 60 minutes or until lattice top is golden brown. Cool. Gently brush lattice top with maple syrup and top with pecan halves. Refrigerate at least one hour before serving. Refrigerate leftovers.

TIP: Cover edge of pie crust with strip of aluminum foil during last 10 to 15 minutes of baking if necessary to prevent excessive browning.

The Pillsbury Company   **Minneapolis, MN**

PUMPKIN PIE FROM FRESH PUMPKIN

Makes 2 9" pies

1 large pumpkin, cut into quarters
2 (12 ounce) cans evaporated milk
4 egs
1½ cups sugar

1 teaspoon salt
2 teaspoons cinnamon
1 teaspoon ginger
½ teaspoon cloves

Remove seeds and pulp from pumpkin. Cover cut sides with plastic wrap and microwave about 20 minutes. Scrape pumpkin pulp from skin and puree in food processor. Measure out 3 cups pureed pulp.

In a mixer bowl, combine all ingredients and beat well. Pour into 2 9" pie crusts. Bake at 425 degrees for 15 minutes, then lower heat to 350 degrees and continue baking for 40 to 60 minutes.

Carol Bender   C. K. McClatchy High School, Sacramento, CA

PECAN PIE

Serves 6 to 8

1 cup white corn syrup
1 cup brown sugar
1/3 teaspoon salt
1/3 cup butter, melted

1 teaspoon vanilla
3 eggs, slightly beaten
1 heaping cup pecan halves
1 unbaked pie crust

Mix syrup, sugar, salt, butter and vanilla. Add slightly beaten eggs. Blend in pecans and pour into an unbaked pie crust. Bake at 350 degrees for 45 minutes.

"No holiday is complete without pecan pie!"

Pat Freshour   Enterprise High School, Redding, CA

PERSIMMON PUDDING (Cake)

1 cup persimmon pulp
1 tablespoon butter, melted
1/4 cup milk
1 teaspoon vanilla
1 teaspoon baking soda
1 cup sugar

1 cup flour
1/2 teaspoon salt
1/2 teaspoon cinnamon
1/2 teaspoon nutmeg
1/2 cup nuts, chopped
1/3 cup golden raisins

In a large bowl, mix persimmon, butter, milk and vanilla. Sift soda, sugar, flour, salt and spices together; stir into persimmon mixture. Stir in nuts and raisins. Turn into a well-greased and floured 1 quart ring mold or bundt pan.* Cover with foil and bake at 350 degrees 50 to 60 minutes or until a toothpick inserted in the middle of the cake comes out clean.

"I double this recipe and use a bundt pan. It takes about 60 minutes."

Ruth Schletewitz   Rafer Johnson Junior High School, Kingsburg, CA

BEST PERSIMMON COOKIES

Makes 3 to 4 dozen

3/4 cup margarine
1 cup sugar
1 teaspoon vanilla
2 eggs
1 cup persimmon pulp
1 teaspoon baking soda

2 cups flour
1 teaspoon cinnamon
1/4 teaspoon allspice
3/4 cup dates, chopped
1/2 cup raisins
1 cup nuts, chopped

Halloween Chicken Pizza Masks, Page 9

Maple Pumpkin Pie, Page 27

California Turkey Breast w/Spinach Dressing, Page 20

Cream margarine, sugar and vanilla. Add eggs and beat. Mix persimmon with baking soda; add to creamed mixture and beat well. Combine flour and spices. Stir in the dates, raisins and nuts. Gradually stir flour mixture into creamed mixture. Drop by teaspoonfuls on a greased cookie sheet. Bake at 375 degrees for 12 to 14 minutes.

"This is Rose Varney's (a retired teacher) recipe. Every fall, she shares persimmons with the teachers and includes her delicious recipe that is a favorite with all!"

Judith Huffman   **Mariposa County High School, Mariposa, CA**

COOKIE CANDY TURKEYS

Serves 12

12 chocolate candy stars
12 caramels, unwrapped

12 scalloped chocolate-frosted
shortbread cookies
12 pieces candy corn

Microwave directions: To make each turkey, place chocolate star, point side up, on work surface. Place one caramel on microwave safe waxed paper; microwave on high for 5 to 10 seconds or until just slightly softened. Place softened caramel on the tip of chocolate star, pressing down so they stick together. To make the tail, press chocolate cookie, striped side facing forward, firmly against the soft caramel to stand upright. Press candy corn on top of caramel to form turkey's beak.

"Very cute. They make great favors for a children's school party."

Laura May   **Hesperia Junior High School, Hesperia, CA**

Thanksgiving

CHRISTMAS

GRAHAM CRACKER GINGERBREAD HOUSE

Makes 1 house

1 10x10 inch piece of cardboard	*"Glue" Frosting*
1 piece of foil	1 egg white
6 graham crackers	1/8 teaspoon salt
1 recipe "glue" frosting	1 cup powdered sugar
1 recipe "butter cream" frosting	1 teaspoon lemon juice

Lightly beat egg white and salt together with electric mixer. As mixture thickens, add powdered sugar gradually and lemon juice. Beat until thick and stiff. Add only as much powdered sugar as needed to make thick and stiff.

"Butter cream" frosting

1 (1 pound) box of powdered sugar	1/4 cup milk
1/4 teaspoon salt	1 teaspoon vanilla

Combine all the ingredients and beat with electric mixer until smooth and creamy. If frosting is too stiff, beat in a few drops of milk, until frosting is spreadable.

1. Make "glue" frosting, set aside.
2. Cover cardboard with foil.
3. Break one whole graham cracker in half; cut the half piece in half (gently with a serrated knife) forming a triangle.
4. Glue two whole graham crackers together to form a "roof."
5. Stand "roof" upright to dry for a few hours.
6. Break one whole graham cracker in half to form the "ends" of the house.
7. Glue two whole graham crackers with 2 half pieces to form "side" walls. Let dry.
8. Make "butter cream" frosting.
9. Frost house and roof together--being VERY careful.
10. Add decorations to house, using "glue" frosting.

Suggested decorations:

M&M plain candies	candy sprinkles
small gum drops	candy corn
red dots	Reese's pieces
miniature jelly beans	licorice
red hots	tube frostings

"This is a lot of fun for teenagers as well as children. Small children will need an adult to put the house together. I do this as a Christmas project in my foods classes."

Vicki Giannetti   **Foothill High School, Sacramento, CA**

HOLIDAY WREATH

Makes one

1 stick margarine
30 to 40 large marshmallows
　(10 g package)
1 teaspoon vanilla

Few drops green food coloring
6 cups corn flakes
Red hot candies

Melt the margarine in a large saucepan over low heat. Add marshmallows, a few at a time, and stir gently until completely melted. Continue heating and stirring about 1 to 2 minutes. Remove from heat. Add vanilla. Add food coloring drop by drop until mixture is grass green. Stir in corn flakes. Drop mixture onto a round glass platter. Grease hands and form a wreath shape. Decorate with red hot candies. Place a red bow at top. Keep in a cool place until ready to serve.

"Visiting relatives or friends at Christmas? Take this with you! It adds a smashing touch for the holidays. Great for potlucks too!"

Sharron Maurice　　　　　　　　　**Blythe Middle School, Blythe, CA**

CRANBERRY ICE A LA' ANN

Serves 4 to 6

2 (12 ounce) packages cranberries
2 cups plus 2 ounces water
cup for cup sugar

½ to ¾ cup lemon juice
2 cups cold water
3 egg whites

Boil cranberries in water for five minutes, then strain and add sugar, equal to the amount of strained sauce. Bring to a boil again, then immediately remove from heat. Add lemon juice and cold water. Put into freezer until partially frozen. When partially frozen, add stiffly beaten egg whites and return to freezer. The ice is best if made the day before.

"This recipe comes from both my husband's family and mine. It's a very special part of our meal."

Lera St. Louis　　　　　　　　　**Buena High School, Ventura, CA**

BANANA FREEZE

Serves 12 to 15

2 cups sugar
3 cups water
2 cups bananas, mashed (4 to 6)
1 (6 oz.) can frozen lemonade
　concentrate

1 (6 oz.) can frozen orange juice
　prepared with 3 cups water
1 quart pineapple juice
2 (2 litre) bottles lemon-lime soda

Combine sugar and water; boil together about 3 minutes. Cool. Mash banana; add to fruit juices and stir in sugar syrup. Pour into containers and freeze. When ready to serve, thaw slightly. Pour carbonated beverage over mixture.

Note: exact proportions are not important. Add more pineapple juice if more guests arrive than you had planned. If too sweet for your taste, add more water.

"To make it festive for Christmas, add red or green food coloring (green works better). You can keep the frozen mixture in the freezer indefinitely. Conveniently made in advance, it can be stored for future use."

Carole Call   **Costa Mesa High School, Costa Mesa, CA**

EGG NOG

½ cup sugar   *⅛ teaspoon salt*
3 egg yolks   *3 egg whites*
¼ teaspoon salt   *¼ cup sugar*
4 cups milk, scalded   *½ teaspoon vanilla*

Beat ½ cup sugar into egg yolks. Add ¼ teaspoon salt and stir in milk slowly. Cook in double boiler until mixture coats a spoon, stirring constantly. Cool.

Add ⅛ teaspoon salt to egg whites and beat until stiff; add remaining ¼ cup sugar; beat well and add to custard mixture along with vanilla. Mix thoroughly and chill.

"If you love egg nog, you'll love this one! This is my husband's favorite."

Charla Rayl   **Fallbrook High School, Fallbrook, CA**

WASSAIL

Makes 27 4-ounce cups

whole cloves   *1 gallon apple cider*
10 2" cinnamon sticks   *1½ cups lemon juice*
6 oranges

Insert cloves into oranges ½-inch apart. Bake, uncovered, in a shallow pan for 30 minutes at 350 degrees. At the same time, heat the cider in a large kettle until bubbles appear at the edges. After bubbles appear remove from heat, add lemon juice, cinnamon sticks and oranges. Cover and heat over very low heat for 30 minutes.

"A Christmas time favorite. I've had the recipe so long I don't even remember where I got it. Enjoy."

Amber Bradley   **Granite Hills High School, El Cajon, CA**

SHRIMP COCKTAIL BEVERAGE

Serves 25 (½ cup servings)

2 (46 oz.) cans tomato juice   *3 tablespoons Worcestershire*
1½ cups catsup   *2 tablespoons prepared horseradish*
1 cup celery, finely chopped   *juice of 1 lemon*
3 tablespoons sugar   *½ teaspoon salt*
2 (4½ oz.) cans shrimp, cleaned, *½ teaspoon garlic salt*
   broken and drained

Combine all ingredients in a gallon container. Refrigerate at least three hours or overnight. Serve cold.

"A favorite at any party I have taken this to."

Kristine Haas   **La Habra High School, La Habra, CA**

CHEESE BALL

Serves 10 to 15

2 (8 ounce) packages cream cheese,   *1 medium onion, chopped*
  softened   *1 teaspoon salt*
1 (10 ounce) package extra sharp   *½ teaspoon pepper*
  Cheddar cheese, grated   *1 cup walnuts, chopped*

Place cream cheese, Cheddar cheese, onion, salt and pepper in a large bowl. Mix together. Place in refrigerator to harden (about 20 minutes). Shape into a ball and roll in chopped nuts.

"This is an excellent tasting cheese ball and so easy to make. Makes a great holiday gift."

Connie Sweet   **Rim of the World High School, Lake Arrowhead, CA**

CHEDDAR CHIVE CHEESE BALL

Makes one

2 cups sharp Cheddar cheese, grated   *12 ounces cream cheese*
2 teaspoons prepared horseradish   *4 tablespoons fresh chives, chopped*
2 to 3 drops liquid smoke   *nuts, chopped*

Cream Cheddar, horseradish, liquid smoke and cream cheese together thoroughly. Add chopped chives and mix in. Put mixture in refrigerator and chill for at least half an hour. Form cheese into a ball and roll in finely chopped nuts.

"This recipe comes from an article I wrote on 'Making Fresh Herb Cheese' for The Herb Companion magazine."

Lynn Alley   **Diegueno Junior High School, Encinitas, CA**

COCKTAIL SHRIMP DIG

Serves 6 to 12

1 (8 oz.) package cream cheese   *bottled cocktail sauce*
1 (6 oz.) canned or fresh shrimp,   *crackers (wafer style are best)*
  cooked

Place cream cheese on a small decorative plate. Drain and rinse shrimp. Sprinkle over cream cheese. Pour desired amount of cocktail sauce over shrimp and cream cheese. To serve: Spread a small amount of appetizer on cracker and enjoy!

"We traditionally enjoy this for Christmas brunch while we are opening presents!!"

DeLisa Davis   **Sutter High School, Sutter, CA**

BAKED BRIE IN PHYLLO

Serves 24 to 30

¼ cup apricot preserves   *½ pound phyllo dough*
2 pound wheel of brie cheese   *½ cup butter, melted*

Spread preserves on top of brie. Wrap brie in thawed phyllo dough, brushing each sheet with melted butter. Turn cheese over after applying a sheet of phyllo dough for even distribution. Brush phyllo wrapped brie with melted butter; cover and refrigerate.

Before serving, place in a shallow baking dish and bake at 425 degrees for 8 to 12 minutes, or until golden brown. Let stand 10 minutes. Serve with baked pita chips.

"Always the hit of the party!"

Pat Curtis   **Ensign Middle School, Newport Beach, CA**

BACON WRAPPED CHESTNUTS

Makes about 48 to 60

2 pounds bacon   *1 cup catsup*
3 cans whole water chestnuts   *½ cup granulated sugar*

Cut bacon in half. Wrap each water chestnut with a ½ strip of bacon. Hold with a toothpick. Bake in 350 degree oven for 45 minutes. Mix together catsup and sugar in an oven-proof serving dish. Place the baked, bacon-wrapped chestnuts in the catsup mixture and put in oven again. Bake an additional 30 minutes at 350 degrees.

"This recipe was given to me by our art teacher, Sue Pedersen."

Susan Lefler   **Ramona Junior High School, Chino, CA**

GERMAN HOLIDAY MEATBALLS

Serves 8-10

½ pound pork sausage   *1 teaspoon prepared mustard*
¼ cup onion, finely chopped   *¼ teaspoon garlic salt*
1 (14 ounce) can sauerkraut, drained   *⅛ teaspoon pepper*
¾ cup + 3 tablespoons fine dry   *¼ cup flour*
*   bread crumbs, divided*   *2 eggs, beaten*
1 (3 ounce) package cream cheese   *¼ cup milk*
2 tablespoons fresh parsley, snipped

Sauté sausage and onion; drain. Add chopped sauerkraut and 3 tablespoons bread crumbs. In another bowl, combine cream cheese, parsley, mustard, garlic salt and pepper; stir into kraut mixture and chill. Form into ¾-inch balls; coat with flour. Combine eggs and milk, then roll floured balls in egg mixture, then roll in remaining bread crumbs. Spear meatballs with fondue fork; heat oil in fondue pot to 375 degrees. Fry meatballs for 30 to 60 seconds each--everyone frying their own.

"My students like these--even with sauerkraut in them. My son brought the recipe home from Germany."

Deanne Moody   **Monte Vista High School, Spring Valley, CA**

QUICHE WEDGES

Makes 12 to 14 servings

1 (10 ounce) package frozen Welch
    rarebit
2 eggs
⅓ teaspoon pepper

5 slices bacon, crisp cooked, drained
    and crumbled
1 9" baked pastry shell
pimiento stars

Defrost frozen rarebit in a 350 degree oven or microwave. Cool slightly. Beat eggs; add rarebit and pepper, mixing until well blended. Stir in bacon and pour mixture into baked pastry shell. Bake in 350 degree oven for 30 minutes or until a knife inserted just off-center comes out clean. Let stand at room temperature for 10 to 15 minutes before serving. Cut into wedges to serve. Top each piece with a pimiento star, if desired. Garnish with fresh parsley sprigs.

"The red pimiento stars and green parsley garnish make this an attractive Christmas party appetizer or snack."

Pat Dallas   **Westminster High School, Westminster, CA**

GIANT OLD-FASHIONED CRANBERRY MUFFINS

Makes 6 large or 12 regular muffins   **Photo on Page 60**

1 package Pillsbury Cranberry Quick
    Bread Mix
½ cup walnuts, chopped
½ cup raisins
¾ cup applesauce
½ cup water
1 egg

1 tablespoon oil
1 teaspoon cinnamon
¼ teaspoon allspice
Glaze
½ cup powdered sugar
2 to 3 teaspoons milk

Heat oven to 400 degrees. Grease bottom of 6-cup large or 12-cup regular muffin pan or line with paper baking cups. In large bowl, combine all muffin ingredients. Stir 50 to 75 strokes by hand until mix is moistened. Divide batter evenly between muffin cups; cups will be full.

Bake at 400 degrees for 20 to 30 minutes or until golden brown. Cool 5 minutes; remove from pan. In small bowl, combine all glaze ingredients until desired drizzling consistency. Drizzle over warm muffins. Store in refrigerator.

HIGH ALTITUDE--Above 3500 feet: Add 2 tablespoons flour to dry mix. Bake as directed.

The Pillsbury Company   **Minneapolis, MN**

TEATIME TASSIES

Serves 24

1 (3 oz.) package cream cheese	*¾ cup brown sugar*
½ cup butter	*1 tablespoon butter, softened*
1 cup flour, sifted	*1 tablespoon vanilla*
1 egg	*⅔ cup pecans or walnuts, broken*

Cheese pastry: Let cream cheese and ½ cup butter soften at room temperature, blend. Stir in flour. Chill slightly for one hour. Shape into 24 1-inch balls. Place in greased muffin cups or small Swedish tart pans. Press dough on bottom and sides of cups.

Nut filling: Beat together egg, brown sugar, 1 tablespoon butter and vanilla until smooth. Put half the nuts into the 24 cups. Add egg mixture and top with the rest of the nuts. Bake at 325 degrees for 25 minutes. Cool and remove from pans.

"These are easy to make and are a gourmet delight!"

Ruthanne Rocha   **South Fork High School, Miranda, CA**

PRIJESNAC (Yugoslavian Cheese Bread)

Serves 15 to 20

4 eggs	*3 tablespoons cottage cheese*
¾ pound Monterey jack cheese,	*3 cups "Bisquick"*
grated	*½ cup plus 1 tablespoon buttermilk*
¾ cube butter, melted	

Beat eggs well. Add jack cheese, cottage cheese, butter, Bisquick, and buttermilk. Stir well. Bake in a well-greased 13"x9¼"x2" pan, at 350 degrees for 45 minutes. Cut into small squares. Serve warm.

"This is a great ethnic favorite we always serve as an appetizer on Christmas which is celebrated on January 7, by the Serbian Orthodox in our hometown of Jackson, CA."

Gerry Banicevich   **Cordova High School, Rancho Cordova, CA**

HOLIDAY BREAD CORNUCOPIAS WITH HAM FILLING

Serves 20

20 slices bread
2 tablespoons butter
1 (3 oz.) package cream cheese,
    softened to room temperature
1 (4½ oz.) can deviled ham
3 tablespoons minced onion

1½ teaspoons horseradish
⅛ teaspoon celery seed
dash of salt and pepper
parsley sprigs
paprika (for color)

Preheat oven to 350 degrees. With 3-inch round cookie cutter, cut 20 bread circles from regular sliced bread. Melt butter. Flatten each circle with rolling pin, brush with melted butter on both sides and roll to form a cornucopia. Fasten with a toothpick. Bake on ungreased cookie sheet for 12 minutes at 350 degrees. At serving time, fill with deviled ham filling.

Deviled ham filling:
Blend together cream cheese and deviled ham, minced onion, horseradish, celery seed, salt and pepper.
Fill the cornucopia shells by teaspoonfuls and garnish with tiny sprigs of parsley at fold of cornucopia. Sprinkle filling with paprika for added color.

"An easy appetizer that tastes as good as it looks. Can be placed on a cake plate and garnished to fit any occasion."

Karen Tilson   **Poly High School, Riverside, CA**

CRANBERRY WALNUT SCONES

Serves 6

3 cups flour
½ cup sugar
1 tablespoon baking powder
½ teaspoon baking soda
½ teaspoon salt
¾ cup butter or margarine, cut into
    small pieces
1 cup fresh or frozen cranberries
½ cup walnuts
1½ teaspoons grated orange peel

1 cup buttermilk
1 tablespoon milk or cream
1 tablespoon sugar mixed with
    ¼ teaspoon ground cinnamon and
    ⅛ teaspoon ground allspice
Whipped Honey Orange Cheese
1 (8 ounce) package cream cheese
2 tablespoons honey
1 tablespoon grated orange peel

In a large bowl, stir together flour, ½ cup sugar, baking powder, baking soda and salt. Using a pastry blender or your fingers, cut or rub butter into flour mixture until coarse crumbs form; stir in cranberries, walnuts and orange peel. Add buttermilk and mix with a fork until dough is evenly moistened.

Gather dough into a ball and place on a floured board. Roll or pat into a ¾-inch thick circle. Using a 2½" cutter, cut into rounds. Place on a greased 12"x15" baking sheet, spacing about 1½ inches apart. Reroll and cut scraps. Brush tops of scones with cream, sprinkle with sugar-spice mixture.

Bake on a lower rack in a 400-degree oven until tops are lightly browned, 14 to 16 minutes. Serve warm with Whipped Honey-Orange Cheese: in a small bowl, beat cream cheese with honey and grated orange peel until light and fluffy. Serve or cover and chill up to 2 days.

"Great for Christmas morning! Serve with oven fried bacon, fruit compote and hot coffee or cocoa."

Kris Hawkins   **Clovis West High School, Fresno, CA**

HOLIDAY SCONES

Serves 4

2 cups flour	*sugar for topping*
½ cup granulated sugar	*1 large egg*
1½ teaspoons baking powder	*1½ teaspoons vanilla*
½ teaspoon baking soda	*½ cup buttermilk*
¼ teaspoon salt	
6 tablespoons very cold butter or	
* margarine*	

In a large bowl, stir together flour, sugar, baking powder, baking soda and salt. Grate the cold butter or margarine over the flour mixture and stir to combine using a fork. In a small bowl, stir together the buttermilk, egg and vanilla. With lightly floured hands, pat the dough to ¾" thick. Cut into squares or triangles. Sprinkle top of scones with sugar. Place 2 inches apart on a lightly greased cookie sheet. Bake at 400 degrees for 10 to 15 minutes, or until lightly browned. Cool for 5 minutes, then transfer to a wire rack. Serve warm with jam and butter.

"This family favorite is great--try adding 1½ cups blueberries (fresh or frozen) when you start to pat the dough out before cutting."

Donna A. Small   **Santana High School, Santee, CA**

GRANDMA'S CINNAMON BREAD

Serves 6 to 8 per loaf

2 cups milk	*½ cup butter, melted*
2 packages dry yeast	*1 cup sugar*
½ cup warm water	*2 teaspoons salt*
7 cups flour (approximate)	*melted butter for topping*
2 eggs, beaten	*3 tablespoons cinnamon*

Scald milk; set aside to cool. Soften yeast in warm water in a large bowl. Let stand 5 minutes. Stir in 4 cups flour, cooled milk, eggs, ½ cup butter, ½ cup sugar and salt. Work in as much flour as needed for a soft dough and knead until smooth. Put in greased bowl, cover and let rise until double. Punch down. Divide dough into 3 parts. Roll first part out into a rectangle. Brush with melted butter. Sprinkle with part of the cinnamon-sugar. Roll up as for a jelly roll. Seal edges and place in 4½"x8½" loaf pan. Repeat with remaining 2 sections of dough. Let rise until double. Bake at 350 degrees for 35 to 45 minutes until golden brown. Brush with melted butter and cool on racks.

"This bread has been a family favorite for many years. It also makes a delicious gift at Christmas."

Wendy Johnson   **Temecula Valley High School, Temecula, CA**

REFRIGERATOR ROLLS

Makes 3 dozen

1 package yeast
¼ cup warm water
1 cup scalded milk (heat 2 minutes in microwave)
¼ cup sugar

¼ cup shortening
1 teaspoon salt
3½ cups flour
1 egg

Soften yeast in warm water, let set. Combine milk, sugar, shortening and salt. Cool to lukewarm.

Add 1½ cups flour--beat well. Beat in yeast and egg. Gradually add enough remaining flour to make a soft dough. Knead 3 to 5 minutes. Place in a greased bowl, turning once to grease the surface. Cover, chill at least 2 hours or up to 4 to 5 days.
Second day:
Let dough set out at room temperature for 1 hour. Shape dough. Let rise by placing in 140 degree oven with door open for 10 to 20 minutes. Bake on greased baking sheet in a hot oven (400 degrees) for 12 to 15 minutes or until light brown.

"This recipe can be made ahead several days before it's needed. Keep it in the refrigerator until needed. Shape it and use the fast rising method and have fresh, home-baked rolls on Christmas or any other holiday."

Janet Griffith   **Norco High School, Norco, CA**

CINNAMON STICKS

Serves 4 to 6

¾ cup sugar
1 tablespoon cinnamon

1 loaf unsliced bread
½ to 1 cup margarine, melted

Place sugar and cinnamon in a brown paper bag and shake together. Set aside. Remove crusts from bread. With bread knife, cut down middle of loaf. Then cut across, making 6 cuts. Brush each "stick" with melted margarine, drop into bag with cinnamon-sugar and shake. Do 4 to 5 sticks at one time. Place on cookie sheet and bake at 350 degrees for 8 to 10 minutes.

"These are inexpensive, quick, delicious and fill the air with a wonderful aroma. Can be made for any holiday, but especially Christmas."

Barbara Ford　　　　　**Cope Junior High School, Redlands, CA**

NORWEGIAN LEFSE

Serves 10 to 12

3 cups mashed potatoes	*1/2 teaspoon salt*
1/4 cup butter or margarine	*1/2 cup cream (half & half)*
1 tablespoon sugar	*1 1/2 cups flour*

Prepare mashed potatoes. Add butter or margarine, sugar, salt and cream. Beat well. Refrigerate two hours. Add flour and form into 2½-inch balls. Roll very thin and bake on a lefse grill (or large electric fry pan) at 500 degrees. Turn only once. Lefse is done when evenly browned.

After the lefse is baked, roll between several layers of paper towels to keep the moisture in. When cool, pack in plastic bags. Serve with butter.

"My students demonstrate foods from their culture in our 'Cultural Bazaar' section. I share this recipe. It's like a Norwegian tortilla!"

Nancy Jordahl　　　　　**Rio Tierra Junior High School, Sacramento, CA**

RED AND GREEN HOLIDAY SALAD

Serves 4

1/2 pound fresh spinach	*1/4 teaspoon pepper*
1 red bell pepper	*6 tablespoons olive oil*
2 tablespoons vinegar	*1/4 cup blue cheese, crumbled*
1/2 teaspoon salt	

Pull the stems from the spinach and wash the leaves. Tear the leaves into pieces. Cut the pepper in strips and add it to the spinach. Shake the vinegar, salt and pepper in a jar. Add the oil and shake again. Crumble the blue cheese and add it to the dressing. Pour the dressing over the salad and toss.

Note: Sweet red pepper and tangy blue cheese compliment spinach beautifully. For an even more colorful salad, combine red and yellow peppers. You can make both the salad and the dressing ahead and combine them at the last moment. Washed and dried spinach will keep overnight. Wrap it in a paper towel, put it in a plastic bag and refrigerate.

"Great for Christmas! Colorful and nutritious! Lots of vitamin A and vitamin C!"

Sue Zallar　　　　　**Capistrano Valley High School, Mission Viejo, CA**

REMBRANDT'S SPINACH SALAD

Serves 4-6

1 bunch fresh spinach
3 ounces blue cheese, crumbled

bacon, fried crisp and crumbled
  (or bacon bits)
Italian dressing

Wash, stem and wrap fresh spinach in paper towels; refrigerate. Fry bacon until crisp; drain and crumble; then add blue cheese and bacon to fresh spinach. Dress with dressing.

"Great with ham; pretty at Christmas."

Libby Bruce   **Troy High School, Fullerton, CA**

4 BEAN SALAD

Serves 12 to 14

1 2-pound can kidney beans
1 2-pound can wax beans
1 2-pound can green beans
1 2-pound can garbanzo beans
1 green pepper, finely chopped
1 small red onion, finely chopped

$^{1}/_{2}$ cup salad oil
$^{3}/_{4}$ cup sugar
1 teaspoon salt
$^{1}/_{2}$ teaspoon pepper
$^{1}/_{2}$ cup vinegar

Drain the beans. Combine the rest of the ingredients and gently stir in the beans. Marinate for at least 24 hours in the refrigerator, stirring several times. To serve, pour off some of the liquid.

"Before my dad passed away, he didn't think that Christmas dinner was complete without this salad. It is colorful, easy to make, tastes great and lasts for days."

Maggy Flath   **Nevada Union High School, Grass Valley, CA**

NANA'S CRANBERRY SALAD

Serves 10

1 quart fresh cranberries
2 oranges, diced (save rind of
  $^{1}/_{2}$ orange)
2 cups sugar

2 envelopes Knox Gelatin
$^{1}/_{4}$ cup water
1 cup celery, diced
1 cup apple, diced

Grind cranberries and the rind of $^{1}/_{2}$ orange. Mix with sugar. Cook for 2 minutes. Soften gelatin in water. Add gelatin to cranberry/sugar mixture. Cool completely. When mixture is cold, add the pulp of oranges, celery and apple. Pour into a mold or pyrex pan and chill.

Susan M. White   **San Dieguito High School, Encinitas, CA**

CRANBERRY JELLO SALAD

Serves 4 to 6

1 (6 ounce) package raspberry Jello (sugar free)
2 cups hot water
1 cup hot cranberry juice (low calorie)

½ cup apple juice
½ cup celery, chopped
½ cup apples, chopped
½ cup orange slices, chopped

Combine Jello, hot water, hot cranberry juice and apple juice. Chill. When mixture begins to gel, add chopped celery, apples and oranges. Chill until completely set.

"This is a very light, easy and yet tasty salad. It is a great accompaniment for traditionally heavy holiday meals."

Evelyn Thomas   **Chaffey High School, Ontario, CA**

DREAM SALAD

Serves 12 to 16

1 (2 pound) can crushed pineapple, drained, liquid reserved
1 small package lemon Jello
8 ounces marshmallows

1 (8 ounce) package cream cheese, softened
1 cup Cool Whip
1 small package cherry Jello

Add water to pineapple juice to make 2 cups of liquid. Bring to a boil; remove from heat and dissolve lemon Jello in this. Stir in the marshmallows until almost melted. Chill until it begins to thicken. In a separate bowl mix cream cheese, pineapple and Cool Whip. Add this to lemon mixture. Pour into a 9"x13" pan and refrigerate until set. Prepare cherry Jello according to package directions. Pour this Jello over the top of the cool pan of Jello mixture. Refrigerate until set.

"I also occasionally put a layer of green Jello on the bottom of the pan to make a 3 layer salad."

Carole DeLap   **Golden West High School, Visalia, CA**

STRAWBERRY JELLO SALAD

Serves 10

1 (6 ounce) box strawberry Jello
1 cup boiling water
2 (10 ounce) boxes frozen strawberries

1 (20 ounce) can crushed pineapple
2 bananas, mashed
1 (8 ounce) carton sour cream

Dissolve strawberry Jello in boiling water. Stir in frozen strawberries until they thaw. Add pineapple and mashed bananas. Pour half of mixture into a 9"x13" baking dish and chill until firm. Frost with sour cream. (It's easier to spread if it has been standing at room temperature a few minutes.) Pour on remaining mixture and chill until firm.

"My four daughters don't feel like it's Christmas unless I serve this salad with Christmas dinner."

Beth Swift   **Buena Park High School, Buena Park, CA**

RASPBERRY JELLO MOLD

Serves 8

2 (6 ounce) packages raspberry Jello
2 cups boiling water
2 (10 ounce) packages frozen
    raspberries
1½ cups to 2 cups crushed
    pineapple

2 to 3 large ripe bananas, sliced
1 cup sour cream
or ½ cup sour cream + ½ cup
    cream cheese
1 cup nuts, chopped

Dissolve Jello in water and add berries, heat until thawed. Add pineapple and bananas. Pour ½ Jello into mold. Chill until partially set. Top with sour cream and nuts, then pour remaining Jello mixture on top.

Donna Fippin   **Bret Harte High School, Altaville, CA**

POMEGRANATE JELLO RING

Serves 12

3 cups boiling water
3 small boxes raspberry Jello
1 large (#2) can crushed
    pineapple

1 package frozen raspberries
1 can whole cranberry sauce
2 cups pomegranate seeds

Add boiling water to Jello in medium-sized bowl and stir until dissolved. Add remaining ingredients, including juices. Pour into a bundt pan. Chill until set.

"Perfect with turkey, festive garnished with mint sprigs. A great recipe from my Silveira relatives in Fresno."

Anne Silveira   **Shasta High School, Redding, CA**

CRANBERRY DELIGHT

Serves 12

1 (4 ounce) can crushed pineapple
2 (3 ounce) packages strawberry Jello
1 (16 ounce) can whole cranberry
    sauce
1 (8 ounce) package cream cheese,
    softened

¼ cup sugar
1 cup evaporated milk
1 teaspoon vanilla
1 tablespoon unflavored gelatin
¼ cup cold water

Drain pineapple, reserving syrup; add water to syrup to make 2½ cups. Place 1¼ cups of syrup mixture in saucepan and bring to a boil. Dissolve 1 package of Jello in boiling syrup mixture. Add ½ drained pineapple and ½ cranberry sauce. Mix well and pour into a 9"x13" dish. Chill until firm.

Beat cream cheese with sugar until smooth. Gradually beat in evaporated milk and vanilla. Soften unflavored gelatin in the cold water and heat to dissolve. Blend gelatin into cheese mixture, pour over firm Jello layer. Chill until firm.

Boil remaining 1¼ cup syrup mixture, dissolve remaining package of Jello, add remaining crushed pineapple and cranberry sauce. Chill until room temperature. Pour VERY GENTLY over cheese layer and chill until firm. Cut into squares.

Rhonda Sack (our secretary)   Home Street Middle School, Bishop, CA

FANCY EGG SCRAMBLE

Serves 8

1 cup Canadian bacon, diced
¼ cup green onions, chopped
3 tablespoons butter or margarine
12 eggs, beaten
1 (3 ounce) can mushroom pieces and
 stems, drained

1 recipe cheese sauce
4 teaspoons butter or margarine
2¼ cups soft bread crumbs (3 slices)
⅛ teaspoon paprika

In a large skillet, cook Canadian bacon and green onion in 3 tablespoons butter or margarine, until onion is tender but not brown. Add eggs and scramble just until set. Fold mushrooms and cooked eggs into cheese sauce. Turn into a 12"x7"x2" baking dish. Combine remaining butter, crumbs and paprika; sprinkle on top of eggs. Cover; chill 30 minutes before serving. Bake, uncovered, at 350 degrees for 30 minutes.

Cheese sauce:

2 tablespoons butter or margarine
2 tablespoons flour
½ teaspoon salt

⅛ teaspoon pepper
2 cups milk
4 ounces American cheese, shredded

Melt butter, blend in flour, salt and pepper. Add milk; cook and stir until bubbly. Stir in cheese until melted.

"Do a day ahead and heat in oven while you open presents!"

Rhonda Nelson   Warren High School, Downey, CA

CHRISTMAS CASSEROLE

Serves 12

10 slices sourdough bread, sliced and
 buttered
1 pound sharp Cheddar cheese, grated
1 quart milk

6 eggs
2 teaspoons dry mustard
1 teaspoon salt
1 pound bacon, cooked and crumbled

Remove crusts and cube the buttered sourdough bread. Place bread in a buttered 9"x13" casserole. Toss with grated cheese. In a bowl, mix together milk, eggs, dry mustard and salt. Pour mixture over bread and cheese. Refrigerate overnight. Bake, uncovered, for 45 minutes at 350 degrees. Top with crisp, crumbled bacon.

"Make this Christmas Eve. Then, bake it while the kids open presents on Christmas morning!"

Paula Skrifvars **Brea Junior High School, Brea, CA**

SPECIAL CHRISTMAS DRESSING

Serves 6 to 8

25 chestnuts, roasted
1 clove garlic, chopped
1 medium onion
olive oil or cooking spray
1½ pounds mushrooms, sliced
1½ cups fresh cranberries, cut
*   in halves*

½ cup dry white wine
1 teaspoon Mrs. Dash, Extra Spicy
season to taste with lemon
*   pepper, savory, and chives*
¾ cup pine-nuts, optional
½ cup pomegranate seeds

Wash and slit each chestnut. Place on a cookie sheet and bake at 350 degrees for 15 to 20 minutes. Shell while warm and cut each into 3 slices. Set aside.

Sauté garlic and onion in olive oil or spray pan with olive oil cooking spray. Cook until onions are transparent. Add mushrooms, cranberries and chestnuts and toss together for 2 to 3 minutes. Add wine, spices, chives and continue cooking for 4 to 5 minutes, stirring frequently. Pine nuts should be added now, if using. When mushrooms are cooked to your preference, remove from heat. Sprinkle pomegranate seeds on top and serve as a side dish to venison, antelope, reindeer (any game meat) or any conventional meat course like pork, lamb, or poultry.

"A truly unusual dressing that will make your Christmas meal memorable. The pomegranates add a touch of festiveness with their bright red color."

Teena Sobey **Chaparral High School, Las Vegas, NV**

HOLIDAY BEEF TIP ROAST

Serves 4 per pound **Photo on Page 60**

2½ to 4-pound beef tip roast
(cap off)

Place beef tip roast, fat side up, on rack in open roasting pan. Insert meat thermometer so bulb is centered in thickest part. Do not add water. Do not cover. Roast in 325 degrees (slow) oven to 5 degrees below desired doneness; 135 degrees for rare; 155 degrees for medium. For a 1½ to 4-pound roast, allow 30 to 35 minutes per pound for rare, or 35 to 40 minutes per pound for medium. Allow roast to stand 15 to 20 minutes before serving. The temperature of the roast will rise 5 degrees during standing to 140 degrees (rare) or 160 degrees (medium).

NOTE: A beef tip roast will yield four 3-ounce cooked servings per pound.

NUTRIENT DATA PER SERVING: 162 calories; 24 g protein; 6 g fat; 2.5 mg iron; 55 mg sodium; 69 mg cholesterol.

BROCCOLI-STUFFED TOMATO CUPS

Serves 6

2 cups broccoli flowerets	½ teaspoon dried rosemary leaves,
6 small tomatoes	crushed
2 large cloves garlic, minced	½ teaspoon lemon pepper
2 tablespoons olive oil	¼ cup Gruyere cheese, shredded

Cook broccoli flowerets in boiling water in medium saucepan 5 to 8 minutes; drain. Meanwhile cut shallow zigzag edge on top edge of tomato, if desired. Scoop out pulp. Cook garlic in oil in large non-stick frying pan 1 minute. Stir in broccoli, rosemary and lemon pepper and cook until heated through. Fill each tomato cup with equal amounts of broccoli mixture (stems down). Sprinkle an equal amount of cheese over broccoli. Place tomato cups in 11¾"x7½" baking dish. Bake in 325 degrees (slow) oven 10 to 15 minutes. Serve tomato cups with roast.

NOTE: Recipe may be doubled

National Live Stock and Meat Board   **Chicago, IL**

CAJUN-STYLE ROAST BEEF w/SWEET & SPICY PEPPER GRAVY

Serves 12

4 pound beef round-tip roast	1 large onion, sliced
1 teaspoon salt	3 cloves garlic, finely chopped
1 teaspoon white pepper	2 jalapeño peppers, finely chopped
¾ teaspoon black pepper	2 tablespoons flour
½ teaspoon red pepper (cayenne)	¼ teaspoon red pepper (cayenne)
½ teaspoon cumin	¼ teaspoon cumin
Gravy:	⅛ teaspoon white pepper
¼ cup oil	⅛ teaspoon black pepper
2 red bell peppers, cut into strips	2 cups beef broth
2 green bell peppers, cut into strips	

Combine seasonings for roast and rub over the surface of the roast. Place in an open, shallow pan. Insert a meat thermometer into thickest part of beef so tip reaches center of roast. Do not add water. Do not cover. Roast at 325 degrees to desired degree of doneness. The meat thermometer will register 140 degrees for rare, 160 degrees for medium and 170 degrees for well done. Allow 26 to 32 minutes per pound, depending on desired doneness. For easier carving, allow to stand in a warm place 15 to 20 minutes after removal from oven. Roasts usually continue to cook after removal from oven. It is best to remove roast when the thermometer registers 5 degrees below temperature of desired doneness.

For gravy: Heat oil until hot. Stir in red and green peppers, onion, garlic and jalapeño peppers. Cook, stirring constantly, until vegetables are crisp-tender. Mix flour, red pepper, cumin, white pepper, and black pepper; sprinkle over pepper mixture. Cook, stirring constantly, about 3 minutes. Stir in beef broth. Cook, stirring occasionally, until mixture thickens and boils. Serve over hot cooked rice and beef.

NOTE: Jalapeño peppers are very hot. Wear rubber gloves when handling. Wash hands well after handling. DO NOT TOUCH EYES AFTER HANDLING PEPPERS.

"This is a fantastic recipe for a tender roast. The gravy is spicy and flavorful--not for the timid. I use mashed potatoes instead of rice."

Myrna Westmoreland   **Grace Davis High School, Modesto, CA**

BURGUNDY BEEF

Serves 10

2 pounds stewing beef
2 cans mushroom soup
2 cups dry sherry

1 package dry onion soup mix
1 (15 ounce) can mushroom pieces

Cut beef into bite size pieces. Mix all ingredients in an ovenproof casserole dish and bake at 325 degrees for 2 hours.
Serve over rice.

Carol Kagy   **Norwalk High School, Norwalk, CA**

CROWN ROAST OF PORK WITH MUSHROOM & BROCCOLI STUFFING

Serves 6 to 8

1 teaspoon parsley, chopped
3 tablespoons flour
1 teaspoon dried thyme leaves
1/4 teaspoon pepper
1 7-pound pork rib crown roast
(about 12 ribs)
1 teaspoon salt
3 tablespoons salad oil

1 large onion, chopped
1 (12 ounce) package mushrooms,
sliced
1 bunch broccoli, cut into 1/2-inch
pieces
6 cups firm white bread, cubed
(about 10 slices)
1/2 cup chicken broth

In a small bowl, mix parsley, flour, thyme leaves and pepper. Rub inside and outside of pork roast with mixture plus 1 teaspoon salt. Place roast, rib-ends down, in a large roasting pan. Roast in 325 degree oven for 2 hours.

Meanwhile, prepare stuffing: In a 12-inch skillet, over medium-high heat, add salad oil; cook onion until tender and golden, stirring occasionally. Add mushrooms, broccoli, ¾ teaspoon salt, ¼ teaspoon thyme and ¼ teaspoon pepper and cook until mushrooms are tender and golden and broccoli is tender. Stir in bread cubes, chicken broth and toss until well mixed.

When pork has roasted 2 hours, remove from oven and turn rib-ends up; fill cavity with stuffing. (Bake any leftover stuffing in small covered casserole during last 40 minutes of roasting time.) Insert meat thermometer between 2 ribs in the thickest part of meat, being careful that pointed end of thermometer does not touch bone. Return roast to oven and continue roasting about 1½ hours or until thermometer reaches 170 degrees (30 to 35 minutes per pound total cooking time). If stuffing browns too quickly, cover with foil.

"This is my family and friends' favorite dinner meal. It is easy and tastes great!"

Linda Brayton　　　　　　　　**Grace Davis High School, Modesto, CA**

MICROWAVE PEANUT BRITTLE

Makes 1 pound

1 cup sugar	*1 tablespoon margarine*
½ cup light corn syrup	*1½ teaspoons baking soda*
1½ cup shelled RAW Spanish peanuts	*1 teaspoon vanilla*

Grease a baking sheet. Combine sugar and corn syrup in a 3-quart casserole or a large Pyrex measuring cup. Stir in peanuts. Microwave at HIGH (100%) until light brown, 8 to 10 minutes, stirring after each 3-minute interval. Stir in remaining ingredients until light and foamy. Quickly spread on greased baking sheet. Spread as thin as possible, for brittle candy. Cool; break into pieces. Store in airtight container.

"My students love to make it for Christmas presents."

Mary Carr　　　　　　　　**Enterprise High School, Redding, CA**

EASY MOCK TOFFEE

Makes about 2 dozen pieces

Saltine crackers	*1 (12 ounce) package chocolate chips*
½ cup margarine	*1 cup walnuts or almonds, chopped*
1 cup brown sugar	

Line a jelly-roll pan with crackers. Melt margarine and brown sugar. Pour over crackers. Bake 5 minutes at 350 degrees. Pour chocolate chips on top immediately and let melt. Spread evenly. Sprinkle chopped nuts on the top and cool until firm. Break into pieces and serve.

"This is a quick, easy recipe that always brings success!"

Joanne Montoy   **Esperanza High School, Anaheim, CA**

WORLD'S BEST PEANUT-BUTTER FUDGE

Serves 32 (2 servings each)

12 ounces chocolate chips   *1 (14 oz.) can condensed milk*
12 ounces peanut butter
(crunchy, if possible)

Place chocolate chips and peanut butter in microwave bowl. Cook on high for about 1 minute (depends on microwave oven) or until chips are melted. Remove from oven. Stir in condensed milk. Pour into 8"x8"x2" lightly-buttered pan (may line pan with foil for easy removal). Slice into one-inch squares.

"A homemaker in Fair Play, CA called me about a recipe that I had in the Lite & Easy Cookbook. She liked my recipe and asked me if I would like an easy, foolproof, handy recipe for fudge. I said 'Sure,' and I've been using this ever since!"

Carole Jackson   **Apple Valley High School, Apple Valley, CA**

WHITE CHOCOLATE TRUFFLES

Makes approximately 2 dozen

1 pound white chocolate   *¾ pound white dipping chocolate*
¾ cup unsalted, sweet butter   *(approximately)*
3 tablespoons water

Melt 1 pound chocolate, butter and water in a double boiler over hot, not boiling, water. When mixture is melted and mixed together, take off heat and beat until mixture thickens. It can be refrigerated to firm up more quickly. When firm, roll into balls about the size of small walnuts. Melt remaining ¾ pound chocolate in a double boiler over hot, not boiling, water. Dip truffles, one at a time, into chocolate. Place on waxed paper. Let cool.

"It is best to use white chocolate with a high cocoa butter content."

Betty Wells   **Oroville High School, Oroville, CA**

FRENCH CHOCOLATES

Makes about 2 dozen

12 ounces semi-sweet chocolate chips
1 cup walnuts
¾ cup sweetened condensed milk
2 teaspoons vanilla

dash salt
coconut
chocolate sprinkles
chopped nuts

In a double-boiler, over hot but not boiling water, add chocolate chips. Stir in 1 cup chopped walnuts, sweetened condensed milk, vanilla and salt. When melted, take off heat. Cool 5 minutes. Shape into 1-inch balls. Roll in finely chopped walnuts, coconut or chocolate sprinkles.

"This is a fool-proof recipe. It tastes like fudge, but even richer."

Linda Winzenread   **Whittier High School, Whittier, CA**

PEANUT BUTTER BALLS

Makes approximately 4 dozen

2 cups peanut butter, creamy or
*   crunchy*
1½ pounds confectioners sugar

1 cup butter or margarine (2 sticks)
2 (8 ounce) Hershey bars
½ bar parafin wax

Cream peanut butter, confectioners sugar and margarine or butter. Roll into ½ to 1" balls. Refrigerate until firm.
Melt Hershey bar and parafin in a double boiler. Dip balls into warm chocolate. Set on wax paper to harden.

"Great with crunchy peanut butter--always the first candy to disappear."

Karen Beigle   **Villa Park High School, Villa Park, CA**

SNO BALLS

Makes 24

2 sticks butter
1 cup sugar
1 (2 pound) can crushed pineapple,
*   drained*
2 beaten egg yolks

2 egg whites
1 cup pecans, chopped
1 box vanilla wafers, broken
*   into pieces*

Cream together butter and sugar. Add drained pineapple and egg yolks. Fold in stiffly beaten egg whites. Add pecans and broken wafers. Mold into 24 balls and refrigerate overnight. The next morning, ice with whipped cream and sprinkle with coconut.

Sharon Topping   **El Rancho High School, Pico Rivera, CA**

RUSSIAN TEA CAKES

Makes approximately 4 dozen

2 cups margarine
1 cup confectioners sugar, sifted
2 teaspoons vanilla

4¹/₂ cups flour
¹/₂ teaspoon salt
1 cup nuts, finely chopped

Mix margarine, sugar and vanilla thoroughly. Measure flour, sift flour and salt together. Blend into creamed mixture. Add chopped nuts. Chill dough.
Heat oven to 400 degrees. Roll dough into 1-inch balls and place on an ungreased baking sheet (cookies do not spread). Bake 10 to 12 minutes or until set but not brown. While still warm, roll in powdered sugar, cool, then roll in sugar again.

Roberta "Bobbette" Smith   **Bear Creek High School, Stockton, CA**

GINGER BALL COOKIES

Makes about 4 dozen

1 cup sugar
1 cup shortening
1 egg
2 tablespoons molasses (yellow label)
1¹/₂ teaspoons soda in a little
*   hot water*

2 cups flour
1 teaspoon cinnamon
1 teaspoon ginger
¹/₄ teaspoon ground cloves

Cream together sugar and shortening. Blend in remaining ingredients. Shape into small balls and roll in granulated sugar before baking. Bake at 350 degrees for about 10 minutes.

"The recipe can be doubled. They are best if not over baked. Remove from oven when very light color and puffy."

Janet Riness   **Westminster High School, Westminster, CA**

CHOCOLATE CRINKLES COOKIES

Makes 6 dozen

¹/₂ cup vegetable oil
4 squares unsweetened chocolate,
*   melted*
2 cups sugar
4 eggs

2 teaspoons vanilla
¹/₂ teaspoon salt
2 cups flour
2 teaspoons baking powder
1 cup powdered sugar

Mix oil, chocolate and sugar. Blend in one egg at a time until well mixed. Add vanilla. Stir in salt, flour and baking powder. Chill overnight.
Preheat oven to 350 degrees. Drop teaspoonfuls of dough into powdered sugar. Roll around and shape into balls. Place about 2 inches apart on greased baking sheets. Bake 10 to 12 minutes.

"A fun and easy recipe for the holidays! Kids love them!"

Linda Woolley   **La Sierra High School, Riverside, CA**

ALMOND CRESCENTS

Makes 2 dozen

1 cup shortening or butter
1/3 cup sugar
2 cups flour
1/4 teaspoon salt

2/3 cup ground blanched almonds
1 cup powdered sugar
1 teaspoon cinnamon

Cream shortening or butter and sugar. Slowly add flour and salt. Stir in almonds. Chill for 2 hours. Shape into crescents. Bake at 325 degrees for 14 to 16 minutes. Cool slightly. Blend powdered sugar and cinnamon together, then roll in powdered sugar and cinnamon mixture.

Jackie Rupp   **Home Street Middle School, Bishop, CA**

MERRY CHOCOLATE NUT CLUSTERS

Makes about 3 dozen   **Photo on Page 61**

1 cup Hershey's Semi-Sweet Chocolate
*   Chips*
1/2 cup Hershey's Vanilla Milk Chips

1 tablespoon shortening
1 (11 1/2 oz.) can lightly-salted
*   peanuts, divided*

In small microwave-safe bowl, place chocolate chips, vanilla milk chips and shortening. Microwave at HIGH (100%) 1 to 1 1/2 minutes or until chips are melted and mixture is smooth when stirred. Reserve 1/4 cup peanuts for garnish; stir remaining peanuts into chocolate mixture. Drop by teaspoonfuls into 1-inch diameter candy papers; top each candy with a peanut. Refrigerate, uncovered, until chocolate is set, about 1 hour. Store in airtight container in cool, dry place.

Hershey Foods Corporation   **Hershey, PA**

SLEEP COOKIES

Makes 1 dozen

2 egg whites
pinch salt
1/4 teaspoon cream of tartar
2/3 cup sugar

1/4 to 1/2 teaspoon vanilla
1 cup chocolate morsels
1 cup pecans, chopped

Preheat oven to 350 degrees. Beat egg whites until foamy. Add salt and cream of tartar; beat until stiff. Add sugar, 2 teaspoons at a time, beating well after each addition. Fold in vanilla, chocolate and nuts. Drop by teaspoonful on a sheet lined with foil. Put in oven and turn off immediately. DO NOT OPEN DOOR for at least 8 hours. Carefully remove from foil.

Cora Lynn Woodall   **Green Valley High School, Henderson, NV**

RUTH HIGGINS' CHRISTMAS COOKIES

Makes about 6 dozen

½ pound margarine
2 cups brown sugar
½ teaspoon salt
2 eggs, separated (Beat egg whites until stiff peaks form)
1 cup candied cherries, finely chopped
1 cup candied pineapple, finely chopped

1 pound dates, pitted and finely chopped
1½ cups walnuts, chopped
4 cups flour, sifted (reserve 1 cup)
1 teaspoon baking soda
1 cup sour milk

Preheat oven to 300 degrees. With an electric mixer, cream margarine and sugar until light. Add 2 egg yolks, beating until fluffy. In a separate bowl, coat chopped fruit and nuts with reserved 1 cup of flour. Sift remaining 3 cups of flour again with baking soda. Add ⅓ of sifted flour and soda to ingredients in mixer. Beat in until blended. Add ½ sour milk, blend. Add ⅓ more flour and soda, blend. Add remaining sour milk and then remaining flour and soda, blending after each addition. Fold in coated fruit and nuts by hand. Lastly, fold in beaten egg whites. Drop by teaspoonfuls onto a greased cookie sheet. Bake 20 to 25 minutes.

"Yummy and plenty to give lots away!"

Alice OKeeffe   **Walnut High School, Walnut, CA**

CHEERY CHOCOLATE TEDDY BEAR COOKIES

Makes about 4 dozen   **Photo on Page 61**

1⅔ cups (10-oz. pkg.) Reese's Peanut Butter Chips
1 cup Hershey's Semi-Sweet Chocolate Chips
2 tablespoons shortening (not butter, margarine or oil)

1 (20 oz.) package chocolate sandwich cookies
1 (10 oz.) box teddy bear-shaped graham snack crackers

Cover tray with wax paper. In medium microwave-safe bowl, place peanut butter chips, chocolate chips and shortening. Microwave at HIGH (100%) 1½ to 2 minutes or until chips are melted and mixture is smooth when stirred. With fork, dip each cookie into chip mixture; gently tap fork on side of bowl to remove excess chocolate. Place coated cookies on prepared tray; top each cookie with graham snack cracker. Refrigerate, uncovered, until chocolate is set--about 30 minutes. Store in airtight container in cool, dry place.

Hershey Foods Corporation   **Hershey, PA**

JOLLY PEANUT BUTTER GINGERBREAD COOKIES

Makes about 6 dozen   **Photo on Page 61**

1²/₃ cups (10-oz. pkg.) Reese's Peanut
   Butter Chips
³/₄ cup (1¹/₂ sticks) butter or
   margarine, softened
1 cup light brown sugar, packed
1 cup dark corn syrup

2 eggs
5 cups all-purpose flour
1 teaspoon baking soda
¹/₂ teaspoon ground cinnamon
¹/₄ teaspoon ground ginger
¹/₄ teaspoon salt

In small microwave-safe bowl, place peanut butter chips. Microwave at HIGH (100%) 1 to 2 minutes or until chips are melted when stirred. In large mixer bowl, beat melted peanut butter chips and butter until well blended. Add brown sugar, corn syrup and eggs; beat until light and fluffy. Stir together flour, baking soda, cinnamon, ginger and salt. Add half of flour mixture to butter mixture; beat on low speed of electric mixer until smooth. With wooden spoon, stir in remaining flour mixture until well blended. Divide into thirds; wrap each in plastic wrap. Refrigerate until dough is firm enough to roll, at least 1 hour.

Heat oven to 325 degrees. On lightly floured surface, roll 1 dough portion at a time to ¹/₈-inch thickness; with floured cookie cutters, cut into Santa or other shapes. Place on ungreased cookie sheet. Bake 10 to 12 minutes or until set and lightly browned. Cool slightly; remove from cookie sheet to wire rack. Cool completely. Frost and decorate as desired.

Hershey Foods Corporation   **Hershey, PA**

SUGAR COOKIES

Makes 5 dozen plus

1 cup butter or margarine
2 cups sugar
³/₄ teaspoons baking soda
¹/₂ teaspoon salt

1 teaspoon vanilla
3 eggs, beaten
3²/₃ cups flour
2 teaspoons baking powder

Cream butter until smooth; add sugar. Beat until creamy. Add baking soda, salt and vanilla to creamed mixture. Beat eggs into creamed mixture. Mix until smooth. Sift together flour and baking powder. Add to creamed mixture. Mix well until smooth. Chill dough several hours or overnight. Roll chilled dough on a lightly-floured board. Cut into shapes, sprinkle with sugar. Place on a lightly-greased cookie sheet and bake at 400 degrees for 5 to 8 minutes.

NOTE: To make your cookies soft, roll them out about ¹/₄-inch thick. Cookies freeze well 2 to 3 weeks.

"My sister got this recipe out of the newspaper several years ago, and we have used it ever since. Everyone loves them."

JoAnn Coleman   **Santa Ana High School, Santa Ana, CA**

CHERRY TARTS

Makes 28

2 (8 ounce) packages cream cheese
¾ cup sugar
1 teaspoon vanilla

2 eggs
1 box vanilla wafer cookies
1 can cherry pie filling

Soften cream cheese; add sugar, vanilla, and eggs beating until well blended. Place one vanilla wafer, rounded side upward, in a decorative paper tart liner. Spoon one tablespoon of the cream cheese mixture on top of each wafer. Top with cherry pie filling; refrigerate for at least 15 minutes.

"A simple yet delightful recipe given to me by my daughter, Audra."

Gerry Henderson   **Temple City High School, Temple City, CA**

SAND TARTS

Makes 4 dozen

1 cup butter
2¼ cups brown sugar
1 egg, plus 1 yolk
4 cups flour, sifted

1 egg white
1 teaspoon cinnamon
2 tablespoons sugar
nuts and cherries for garnish

Preheat oven to 350 degrees.
Cream butter and sugar. Add egg plus yolk and mix well. Blend in flour thoroughly. Roll to ⅟₁₆-inch thickness and cut into desired shapes. Place on an ungreased cookie sheet. Brush with egg white. Blend together cinnamon and sugar; sprinkle on top of tarts. Garnish with nuts and cherries, and bake for 10 to 12 minutes.

"An old family favorite that my mother always made at Christmas time."

Carol O'Keefe   **Canyon High School, Anaheim, CA**

MOM'S CHRISTMAS COOKIES

Serves many!

4 cups flour, sifted
½ teaspoon salt
1 teaspoon baking soda
½ cups sugar

1 cup shortening
3 eggs
1 teaspoon vanilla
½ teaspoon lemon extract

Sift together the flour, salt and soda. Cream together sugar, shortening, eggs, vanilla and lemon extract. Combine the two mixtures. Shape the dough into a roll, 3 inches in diameter. Wrap in wax paper. Chill. Cut roll into slices ½-inch thick. Roll dough about ⅛ inch thick. Cut into shapes with cookie cutters. Bake on lightly greased cookie sheet for 8 to 10 minutes at 350 degrees.

"My mom has been making these every Christmas since I was a very small child!"

Julie Blanchard   **Western High School, Anaheim, CA**

HOLIDAY BELLS

Makes about 48

¾ cup margarine or butter
¼ teaspoon salt
⅔ cup granulated sugar
1 egg

¼ teaspoon coconut flavoring
1¾ cup flour
red or green colored sugar
red and green M&M's

In a large mixer bowl, beat margarine or butter and salt with an electric mixer on medium speed for 30 seconds. Add sugar and beat until fluffy. Add egg and coconut flavoring, beat well. Add flour and beat until well mixed. Cover and chill about 30 minutes or until easy to handle.

Divide dough in half. Shape into two 6-inch rolls. Roll each half in colored sugar. Wrap tightly and freeze until dough is firm (about 4 to 6 hours). To bake, let rolls stand at room temperature for 5 minutes. Cut into ¼-inch thick slices. Let stand 10 minutes to soften. Place on an ungreased cookie sheet. Place an M&M candy on the bottom half of each slice (for bell clapper). Fold in sides, overlapping at top and slightly covering candy. Bake at 350 degrees for 10 to 12 minutes or until edges and bottoms are very lightly brown. Remove and cool on a wire rack.

"Crisp, sugar-edged cookies with colorful candy clappers always look pretty on a cookie tray."

Mary Coffman   **Clovis West High School, Fresno, CA**

LEBKUCHEN ALA KATIE

Makes 42

1 egg, beaten
¾ cup brown sugar, packed
1 cup honey
¾ cup molasses
½ teaspoon grated lemon peel
2 teaspoons lemon juice
4 cups flour
1 teaspoon ground cinnamon

½ teaspoon baking soda
½ teaspoon ground cloves
½ teaspoon ground ginger
Lemon Glaze:
1 egg white, beaten
1 tablespoon lemon juice
dash salt
1½ cups powdered sugar, sifted

In a bowl, combine egg and brown sugar. Beat until light and fluffy. Mix in honey, molasses, lemon peel, and lemon juice. Mix well. Stir together flour, cinnamon, baking soda, cloves and ginger. Blend into molasses mixture. Chill several hours. Divide dough in half.

On a lightly floured surface, roll each half to a 14"x9" rectangle; cut into 3"x2" cookies. Bake on a lightly greased cookie sheet at 350 degrees for about 12 minutes. Cool slightly; remove from cookie sheet and cool on rack. While warm, brush with glaze.

To prepare Glaze: In a bowl, combine egg white, lemon juice and salt. Stir in sifted powdered sugar and beat until smooth.

"My eleven-year-old daughter adjusted Lebkuchen or ginger cookie to her own taste. It is a perennial favorite among midwestern German-Americans, especially at Christmastime. She served it to her German class and everyone loved it!"

Brenda Burke   **Mt. Whitney High School, Visalia, CA**

PERSIMMON PUDDING

Makes 2 to 3 loaves

3 tablespoons butter
1 cup sugar
1 cup flour
1 teaspoon cinnamon
1 teaspoon baking soda

1 teaspoon baking powder
¼ teaspoon salt
1 cup dates, chopped
1 cup persimmon pulp
1 teaspoon vanilla

Cream butter and sugar. Stir in remaining ingredients. Slightly grease 2 pint-sized peanut cans. Fill two-thirds full. Seal well with foil. Put cans in a pan of hot water and bake at 350 degrees for 2 hours (keep adding boiling water to pan). This can be kept in the refrigerator for 2 months, wrapped well in wax paper and foil.

"This can also be baked in 3 small loaf pans--7⅜"x3⅝"x2½," but nothing larger."

Donna Swennes   **El Capitan High School, Lakeside, CA**

STEAMED CRANBERRY PUDDING

Serves 6

2 cups raw cranberries, chopped
1⅓ cups flour
½ teaspoon salt
1 teaspoon soda
¼ teaspoon cinnamon
¼ teaspoon mace
⅓ cup hot water

½ cup light molasses
Supreme Sauce:
1 cup sugar
1 cup light cream
⅓ cup butter
½ teaspoon vanilla

Add cranberries to sifted dry ingredients. Add water and molasses, mix well. Fill greased 1-pound coffee can or pudding mold ⅔ full, cover and steam two hours. Serve with Supreme Sauce--combine sugar, light cream and butter in double boiler. Heat until well blended. Add vanilla. Serve warm over pudding.

Nancy Earnest   **Victor Valley High School, Victorville, CA**

MEXICAN ALMENDRADO WITH CUSTARD SAUCE

Serves 8 to 10

1 tablespoon gelatin
1/4 cup cold water
1/4 cup boiling water
6 egg whites
1 1/2 cup sugar
1 teaspoon vanilla
1/2 to 1 cup almonds, chopped
food coloring--green and red

Custard Sauce:
6 egg yolks
1 quart milk
1/2 teaspoon salt
1/2 teaspoon almond extract
1 teaspoon vanilla
1/2 cup sugar

In a large glass bowl, mix the gelatin with the cold water; add the boiling water and dissolve well. Let cool. In another bowl, beat the egg whites until they are stiff, gradually add the sugar and vanilla. Slowly beat in the cold melted gelatin; when the mixture stands in peaks, divide into 3 equal parts. To one part add 1/2 of the almonds; to each of the other parts add the food coloring, one red, one green. For an added almond taste, add the remaining almonds to the pink and green portions. Line a 9"x13" pan with wax paper, letting it extend above the sides to assist in removing when almendrado gets chilled. Into the pan, alternate the three colors into three layers; the almond mixture should be in the middle. Place in refrigerator for about 4 hours so that it will stiffen. Drizzle custard sauce over the top if desired.

Custard Sauce: Mix all ingredients except vanilla; strain. Cook in a double boiler, stirring constantly until the mixture coats the spoon. Cool; add vanilla.

"This low calorie dessert is perfect alone after a big holiday meal, but it's especially great served with a tray of Christmas cookies."

Shirley Blough   **Hillside Junior High School, Simi Valley, CA**

CHRISTMAS PLUM PUDDING

Serves 14

1 envelope Knox Gelatin
1 cup cold water
1 1/2 squares unsweetened chocolate
1 cup sugar
1 pint (2 cups) milk
1 cup seedless raisins

1/2 cup currants
3/4 cup dates, chopped
1 pinch salt
1/2 teaspoon vanilla
1/2 cup nuts, chopped
3 egg whites, beaten

Christmas

Soften gelatin in cold water for ten minutes. Melt chocolate with part of the sugar; add a little of the milk making a smooth paste. Put remainder of milk in a double boiler; add raisins and chopped fruit. When hot, add melted chocolate, remaining sugar, salt and gelatin. Remove from heat. When mixture begins to thicken, add vanilla and nuts. Fold in beaten egg whites. Pour into a jello mold and refrigerate until firm. Serve with a hard sauce or whipped cream.

"An old family recipe from my mother-in-law. We always serve it at Christmas."

Theresa M. Campbell   **John F. Kennedy High School, La Palma, CA**

MOZART'S MADNESS

Serves 24

1 package (pudding in mix) chocolate cake mix
1 teaspoon ground cinnamon
1 cup sour cream
4 large eggs
½ cup oil

1 (4 oz.) package instant chocolate pudding
½ cup warm water
⅓ cup "Mozart" chocolate liquer
1 (12 oz.) package chocolate chips (semi-sweet)

Combine in bowl: cake mix, cinnamon, sour cream, eggs, oil, pudding mix, warm water and Mozart liquer. Stir to blend, then beat 3 minutes at medium speed. Stir in chocolate chips.

Turn into a greased and floured 10-inch bundt pan and bake 45 to 55 minutes at 350 degrees.

Let cool 20 minutes before removing from pan.

"A cake so truly delicious and moist, you can serve as is or serve with Mozart frosting. A magnificent addition to any holiday sweet table."

Donna Collier   **John Muir Middle School, Burbank, CA**

MOZART'S MADNESS FROSTING

Serves 24

1 (8 oz.) package cream cheese
1 (1 lb.) box powdered sugar
¼ cup "Mozart" liquer

1 (12 oz.) bag semi-sweet chocolate chips

In a bowl combine: cream cheese, powdered sugar and liquer. Beat until smooth and creamy. Melt chocolate chips in the microwave on 50 percent power until creamy. Immediately mix into the frosting and continue beating until well blended. Pour over Mozart's Madness Cake and chill.

"Delicious as frosting on the cake, but this is also a wonderful center for dipped chocolates."

Donna Collier   **John Muir Middle School, Burbank, CA**

Giant Old-Fashioned Cranberry Muffins, Page 36

Holiday Beef Tip Roast with Broccoli-Stuffed Tomato Cups, Page 46, 47

Merry Chocolate Nut Clusters, Page 53, Gingerbread Cookies, Page 55
Chocolate Popcorn Balls, Page 4, and Teddy Bear Cookies, Page 54

MINT CHOCOLATE MOUSSE DESSERT

Serves 16 to 18

Crust:
2 cups vanilla wafer crumbs (about
60 wafers)
1/3 cup butter, melted
Filling:
1 (8 ounce) package cream cheese,
softened
2 cups powdered sugar

3 ounces unsweetened chocolate,
melted
3 eggs
1/2 gallon (8 cups) pink peppermint
ice cream, slightly softened
Topping:
1 cup Satin Fudge Sauce
if desired (refer to next recipe)

Heat oven to 350 degrees. In a small bowl, combine wafer crumbs and butter; mix well. Press crumbs in bottom of ungreased 9"x13" pan. Bake at 350 degrees for 10 minutes or until lightly browned. Meanwhile, beat cream cheese in a small bowl. Add powdered sugar; beat until smooth. Add chocolate; beat well. Add eggs, one at a time, beating well after each addition. Pour over baked crust. Bake at 350 degrees for 12 to 15 minutes or until filling is set. Cool completely.

Spread softened ice cream over chocolate filling; cover and freeze 4 hours or until firm. Let stand at room temperature 10 minutes before serving. Heat fudge sauce until warm. Cut dessert into squares; drizzle warm fudge over each square.

"This is great for Christmas Day because it can be made ahead and just pulled out of the freezer 10 minutes before serving. Tastes great, and it's pretty!"

Shirley Marshman   **West Middle School, Downey, CA**

SATIN FUDGE SAUCE

Makes 1⅔ cups

4 ounces semi-sweet chocolate,
chopped
1/3 cup butter or margarine

1 1/2 cups powdered sugar
1 (5 ounce) can evaporated milk
1 teaspoon vanilla

In a heavy saucepan, combine all ingredients except vanilla. Bring mixture to a boil over medium heat, stirring constantly. Reduce heat to low; cook 5 minutes, stirring constantly. Remove from heat; stir in vanilla. Serve warm over ice cream or desserts. Store in refrigerator.

Shirley Marshman   **West Middle School, Downey, CA**

CHRISTMAS PIE

Serves 8

1 quart peppermint ice cream,
　softened
1 9-inch pastry, chocolate cookie
　or graham cracker crust
1/2 pint hot fudge sauce

Peppermint Meringue:
3 egg whites
1/2 teaspoon vanilla
1/4 teaspoon cream of tartar
6 tablespoons sugar
1/4 cup candy canes, crushed

Spread half of the softened ice cream in pie shell. Cover with fudge sauce. Cover with rest of ice cream. Add more fudge sauce, if desired. Freeze overnight or until firm. Just before serving, make meringue. Beat egg whites with vanilla and cream of tartar until soft peaks form. Gradually beat in 6 tablespoons sugar. Beat until stiff peaks form. Stir in 3 tablespoons crushed peppermint candy. Spread meringue over pie; seal to edge. Sprinkle with 1 tablespoon crushed candy. Place pie on wooden board. Bake until meringue is golden (about 6 minutes) at 400 degrees.

"If you make it once, you will be making it every year...'But Mom, it's tradition!'...the freezer went out one year and everyone wailed because there was no pie!"

Judy Betz　　　　　**Greenfield Junior High School, Bakersfield, CA**

JILL'S CRANBERRY PIE

Serves 8

Filling:
3 cups fresh or frozen cranberries,
　and/or 1 package
1/2 cup sugar
1/2 cup walnuts, chopped

Topping:
2 eggs
1 cup sugar
1 cup flour
1/2 cup butter, melted

Rinse and drain cranberries. Spread over bottom of a greased 10" pie pan. Sprinkle with sugar, then walnuts. For topping, beat eggs; gradually add and beat in sugar. Mix in flour and melted butter. Bake at 375 degrees for 1 hour.

"This is my sister's traditional Christmas dessert. She says it's best served warm with vanilla ice cream."

Diedre Goodnough　　　　　**Norwalk High School, Norwalk, CA**

FAYE'S PUMPKIN CAKE ROLL

Serves 8-12

3 eggs
1 cup sugar
²/₃ cup pumpkin
1 teaspoon lemon juice
³/₄ cup flour
1 teaspoon baking powder
2 teaspoons cinnamon
1 teaspoon ginger

¹/₂ teaspooon nutmeg
¹/₂ teaspoon salt
1 cup walnuts, finely chopped
Filling:
1 cup (or more) powdered sugar
1 (8 ounce) package cream cheese
¹/₄ cup butter
1 teaspoon vanilla

Beat eggs on high speed for five minutes. Gradually beat in sugar. Stir in pumpkin and lemon juice. In another bowl, stir together flour, baking powder, spices and salt. Fold this mixture into the pumpkin mixture. Spread into a greased and floured jelly-roll pan (15"x10"x1"). Top with chopped walnuts. Bake at 375 degrees for 15 minutes. Turn out on towel sprinkled with powdered sugar. Starting at narrow end, roll towel and cake together. Cool. Unroll. Combine filling ingredients and beat until smooth. Spread over cake. Roll and chill. (I think it's best if it is frozen until 20 minutes before serving--it's easier to slice and serve.")

"This is my sister's recipe--I won't fly home for Christmas if she doesn't make this!"

Donna Wendt   **Mt. Carmel High School, San Diego, CA**

ICE CREAM CAKE

Serves 10 to 12

1 angel food cake
1 pint raspberry sherbet

1 pint lime sherbet
1 quart strawberry ice cream

Cut angel food cake into three layers. Remove top two layers. Soften raspberry sherbet and spread evenly on top of bottom cake layer. Place middle cake layer over sherbet layer and freeze until set. Soften lime sherbet and spread evenly on top of middle cake layer. Place top cake layer over sherbet layer and freeze until set. Soften strawberry ice cream and frost top and sides of cake. Freeze until set. Slice when ready to serve.

"This dessert can be adapted to any special occasion with different selections of sherbets and ice cream."

Judy Banks   **Temecula Valley High School, Temecula, CA**

INEXPENSIVE FRUITCAKE

Makes 2 loaves

1½ cups seedless raisins
1½ cups dates, cut up
2 cups sugar
2 cups boiling water
5 tablespoons shortening
3 cups flour, sifted

1 teaspoon baking soda
2 teaspoons cinnamon
1 teaspoon cloves
1 teaspoon salt
1 cup nuts, chopped
1 cup mixed candied fruit

In a saucepan, gently simmer raisins, dates, sugar, boiling water and shortening for 20 minutes. Cool.

Sift together flour, baking soda, and spices. Add to the cooled mixture. Mix in nuts and candied fruit. Pour into two loaf pans or 1 angel food cake pan and bake in preheated 325 degree oven for 1½ to 1¾ hours.

NOTE: Store for several days--always freezes well for the next holiday season.

"Thank you, Beryl, for this recipe. Everyone enjoys this fruitcake."

Signe A. Buckley   **Moore Middle School, Redlands, CA**

HOLIDAY CAKE

Serves 20

¼ pound margarine
1⅓ cup white sugar
2 eggs
2 cups flour
1 teaspoon baking soda
1 teaspoon ground cinnamon
½ teaspoon ground nutmeg

⅓ teaspoon ground cloves
¼ teaspoon baking powder
1 cup nuts, chopped
1 cup raisins
½ cup glazed fruit, chopped
1 cup unsweetened applesauce

Cream together margarine, sugar and eggs. Sift together flour, baking soda, cinnamon, nutmeg, cloves and baking powder. Mix nuts, raisins, glazed fruit with flour mixture. Mix fruit and flour mixture together; add applesauce and mix well. Pour into a greased and floured loaf pan (9"x5"x2¾"). Bake for 1 hour 30 minutes at 350 degrees.

"This is a cake that my grandmother--then a mother--used to make. Now I give to special friends during the holiday season!"

Anita Redman   **John Muir Middle School, Burbank, CA**

MABEL'S SPICE FRUIT CAKE

Serves 10-12

1½ teaspoons baking soda
½ cup sour milk
2½ cups flour
1 cup raisins
1 cup currants
2 teaspoons cinnamon
1 teaspoon ground cloves

1 teaspoon nutmeg
¼ teaspoon mace
1½ cups light brown sugar
½ cup butter or margarine, softened
1 egg
½ cup molasses

Dissolve baking soda in sour milk. Mix together flour, fruit and spices. Then, combine all remaining ingredients in order listed. Spread batter in greased bundt or tube pan and bake at 350 degrees. Bread is done when toothpick placed in the center comes out clean. Check for doneness at 40 minutes, continue baking as needed. Cool and slice thinly.

NOTE: Currants work best but may be hard to find in local stores.

"This is the one fruitcake people don't give away. (Even the males in the family eat this one!)"

Janet Policy　　　　　　　　　　　**Ramona High School, Riverside, CA**

GRANDMA POWELL'S PRUNE CAKE

Serves 6 to 8

1 cup real butter
2 cups sugar
2 cups water
2 tablespoons vanilla
3 cups pitted prunes, diced

2 eggs
3 cups flour
2 teaspoons baking soda
1 teaspoon salt
2 cups walnuts, chopped

In a large saucepan, melt the butter, sugar, water and vanilla over low heat. Add diced prunes. Mix in eggs.

Sift the dry ingredients together and add, a little at a time, to liquid mixture. Mix well with an electric mixer. Add nuts. Place in a greased and floured tube or bundt pan and bake at 425 degrees for 30 minutes, then reduce heat to 375 degrees and bake 10 to 15 minutes more. Cool slightly and remove from pan.

"This recipe is great with a cream cheese glaze and can be decorated with nuts, cherries, etc., for Christmas."

Dianne Sheats　　　　　　　　　　　**Gridley High School, Gridley, CA**

　　　　　　　　　　　Christmas

POPCORN CAKE

Serves 8

3 quarts popped popcorn
1 (14 ounce) package M&M candies
·1 package gumdrops
1 1/2 cups unsalted roasted peanuts
1 1/2 cups roasted pecans

1/2 cup vegetable oil
1/2 cup margarine
1 (16 ounce) bag miniature
   marshmallows

Mix first five ingredients in a large bowl. Melt oil and margarine together, then add marshmallows and stir until marshmallows are melted and creamy. Pour cream mixture over dry ingredients until well coated. Pour into well-greased tube pan and let set overnight. Remove from pan. For Christmas, use red and green M&M's and gumdrops.

"Good recipe for kids!"

Val Herford   **Mesa Intermediate School, Palmdale, CA**

HOLIDAY GIFT CAKE

Serves 10 to 12

1 (8 ounce) package cream cheese
1 cup margarine
1 1/2 cup granulated sugar
1 1/2 teaspoon vanilla
4 eggs
2 1/4 cups sifted cake flour

1 1/2 teaspoon baking powder
3/4 cup maraschino cherries, well
   drained and chopped
1/2 cup pecans or walnuts, chopped
1 1/2 cup sifted confectioners sugar
2 tablespoons milk

Combine softened cream cheese, margarine, sugar and vanilla, mixing until well blended. Add eggs, one at a time, mixing well after each addition. Gradually add 2 cups flour, sifted with baking powder, mixing well after each addition. Toss remaining 1/4 cup flour with cherries and chopped nuts; fold into batter. Pour 1 1/2 cups batter into four greased and floured 1 pound shortening cans, or 1 greased 10" bundt or tube pan. Bake shortening cans for 1 hour and bundt or tube pan for 1 hour and 20 minutes at 325 degrees. Cool for 10 minutes; remove from pan or cans. Cool thoroughly. Glaze with a mixture of confectioners sugar and milk. Garnish with cherries and nuts if desired.
(Kraft Foods Corporation)

"A pretty and delicious dessert. This is my family's favorite for Christmas."

Darlene V. Brown   **Golden Valley Middle School, San Bernardino, CA**

NEW YEARS

DESIGNATED DRIVER DRINKS

Makes 1 serving each

Sunriser

8 to 10 ounce tumbler, filled with
   cracked ice
1 part orange juice
1 part pineapple juice

3 tablespoon grenadine syrup
pineapple wedge and orange slice
   for garnish

Pour equal parts orange juice and pineapple juice into glass. Trickle grenadine into juices until a delicate pink layer forms on bottom. DO NOT STIR. Serve with sip-stick and garnish with pineapple wedge and orange slice.

Club Soda Squeeze

10 to 12 ounce tall glass, filled with
   cracked ice

Club Soda
Lime, cut into quarters

Fill glass with club soda and squeeze quarter of lime into glass. Drop lime quarter into glass and serve with sip-stick.

Shirley Temple

10 to 12 ounce tall glass, filled with
   cracked ice
¾ ounce grenadine syrup

1 part 7-Up
cherry for garnish

Pour grenadine over ice. Fill with 7-Up. Garnish with cherry and serve with sip-stick.

Toxic-Waste Dump

9 to 10 ounce bucket
1 scoop lime sherbet
Lime soda (not 7-Up or Lemon-Lime
   soda)

cherry for garnish

Place 1 scoop lime sherbet in wide mouth glass. Fill with lime soda. Let it foam; add a cherry and serve with a spoon/straw.

Bartman

10 to 12 ounce tumbler
1 scoop vanilla ice cream

Root Beer

Place 1 scoop vanilla ice cream in glass. Fill with root beer. Serve with spoon/straw.

Dan Salisbury and Chuck Hulen
North Orange County Community College District, Adult Education
Vocational Bartending (available at Cypress College)

"These recipes were a great success for the classroom demonstration provided by Dan and Chuck. We also use them at home when guests want a choice."

Donna Hulen   **Los Alamitos High School, Los Alamitos, CA**

CHINESE CHICKEN WINGS

20 chicken wings (about 4 pounds)
½ cup soy sauce
½ cup lemon juice
½ cup molasses

2 garlic cloves, crushed
3 tablespoons salad oil
lemon slices and fresh parsley for
  garnish

Cut chicken wings at joint, discarding tips. In a rectangular baking dish, mix remaining ingredients. Marinate chicken for several hours or overnight. Bake chicken wings at 425 degrees in marinade for 10 minutes. Reduce heat to 350 degrees, bake another 15 minutes or until tender, basting occasionally with marinade. Garnish with lemon slices and parsley.

"This simple, make-ahead recipe is great for entertaining. It multiplies beautifully for a large crowd."

Sue Hope   **Lompoc High School, Lompoc, CA**

PEPPERONI PIZZA DIP

Serves 12

1 (8 oz.) package cream cheese
½ cup sour cream
1 teaspoon oregano
¼ teaspoon garlic powder
⅛ teaspoon crushed red pepper

½ cup pizza sauce
½ cup pepperoni, chopped
¼ cup green onions, sliced
¼ cup green pepper, chopped
½ cup mozarella cheese, grated

In a small mixing bowl, beat together the cream cheese, sour cream, oregano, garlic powder and red pepper. Spread evenly in a 9 or 10 inch dish. Spread a layer of pizza sauce over the top. Sprinkle the pepperoni, green onions, and green pepper onto the pizza sauce. Bake at 350 degrees for 10 minutes. Top with mozarella cheese; bake 5 minutes more, or until cheese is melted. Use as a dip with crackers or broccoli flowerets, red and green pepper strips.

"This is as good as pizza!"

Pat Smith   **Kern Valley High School, Lake Isabella, CA**

SEAFOOD DIP

Makes about 12 cups

1 (28 oz.) can tomato puree
1 (1 1b. 10 oz.) bottle catsup
1 (4 oz.) can sliced olives, drained
1 (4 oz.) can mushrooms, drained
1 jar marinated artichoke hearts,
  drained
1 large can shredded crab, drained
2 cans tiny shrimp, drained
1 can minced clams with juice

1 (15.5 oz.) jar gardiner mixed
  vegetable pickles, cut up
1 (4 oz.) can mild chilies, diced
1 tablespoon sugar
1 tablespoon dried onions
4 dashes vinegar
2 garlic cloves, crushed or garlic
  powder

Mix all ingredients and refrigerate overnight.

"I have the greatest Mom! She's Laura Keiser from Sanger; she loves easy recipes and knows I do too!! She gave me this recipe that everyone who likes seafood loves. The recipe makes lots and freezes very well indefinitely, when stored in glass jars. Thanks Mom!"

Cheryl Mc Daniels   **Green Valley High School, Henderson, NV**

CHEDDAR FONDUE APPETIZER CUBES

Makes 8 dozen

1 long loaf (1 pound) French bread, unsliced, 1 to 2 days old
½ cup butter or margarine
1 (8 ounce) package cream cheese
½ pound sharp cheddar cheese, shredded

¼ teaspoon garlic or onion powder (optional)
2 egg whites, stiffly beaten

Cut the untrimmed bread into cubes about ¾ inch square; set aside. Meanwhile in the top of a double boiler, melt the butter and cream cheese over gently boiling water. Gradually add the shredded cheese, stirring until melted and smooth. Also stir in the garlic or onion powder if used. Remove from heat and quickly fold in the beaten egg whites. Keeping the top of the double boiler over the hot water, use 2 forks (fondue forks work well) to quickly dip cubes in the cheese, coating them evenly. Tap fork lightly, then place cubes slightly apart on waxed paper or greased baking sheets. If cheese becomes too thick to coat the last cubes, place double boiler over heat just to warm cheese. Let coated cubes stand, uncovered, until dry to the touch, about 2 ½ hours. If desired, freeze until firm, then package airtight. To serve, place desired number of cubes (unthawed if frozen) on an ungreased baking sheet. Bake at 350 degrees in the middle section of the oven for about 6 to 8 minutes, until lightly browned, or until hot.

Gwen Hansen   **Bloomington High School, Bloomington, CA**

CHEESE BALL

2 cups cheddar cheese, shredded
3 ounces cream cheese
3 tablespoons mayonnaise
½ teaspoons Worcestershire sauce
dash of onion salt

dash of garlic salt
dash of celery salt
¼ cup black olives, chopped
3 tablespoons parsley, minced
3 tablespoons pecans, chopped

Combine cheeses, mayonnaise, Worcestershire sauce, and spices; beat until smooth. Add olives. Cover and chill until firm. Shape into a ball and roll in pecans and parsley. Cover and chill.

Jeanne Donadio   **Rancho High School, N. Las Vegas, NV**

SHRIMP MOLD

Serves 12

1 can cream of mushroom soup
1 (6 ounce) package of cream cheese
1 envelope gelatin
3 tablespoons water
1 cup mayonnaise

1 cup celery, diced
2 green onions, chopped
1 (6 ounce) can shrimp, chopped
1 baguette or sourdough french bread

In a saucepan, warm soup and cream cheese. Add gelatin and water. Remove from heat and add mayonnaise, celery, onions and shrimp. Mix together and pour into a mold. When thoroughly chilled, serve with sliced baguette or sourdough bread.

"This recipe is always a hit -- anytime!"

Anita Huckert   **Greenfield Junior High School, Bakersfield, CA**

STUFFED MUSHROOMS

Serves 6 to 7

fresh mushrooms (about 25
   ½ dollar size)
4 to 5 tablespoons bacon bits
3 green onions, chopped

1 (8 ounce) package cream cheese,
   softened
½ cup cheddar cheese, grated

Wash mushrooms and remove stem from center. Place upside down on a cookie sheet. Chop stems. In a small bowl, mix stems, bacon bits, green onions and both cheeses. Spoon mixture into each mushroom. Bake at 350 degrees for 15 minutes.

"Easy to prepare -- can be done ahead of time and refrigerated. Bake when ready to serve."

Trena Becker   **Ball Junior High School, Anaheim, CA**

WON TON APPETIZERS

Makes approximately 1-2 dozen

1 package won ton wrappers
corn oil
1 pound hamburger
1 onion, minced
1 package taco seasoning mix

1 small can sliced olives
1½ cups cheddar cheese
1½ cups jack cheese
sour cream

Brush won ton wrappers with oil (a small paint brush works great). Press into a small muffin tin to form a basket. Bake at 350 degrees until lightly browned (about 5 to 10 minutes). Remove from pan and place on cookie sheet. Brown hamburger with onion. Add taco seasoning mix and follow directions on back of mix. Remove from heat and place in bowl. Add olives and cheese. Fill won ton wrapper baskets with meat and cheese mixture. Broil until cheese melts. Dot with sour cream.

Penney Childers   **Ramona High School, Ramona, CA**

EGG ROLLS

Makes 50 to 60

3 pounds ground beef
4 eggs
1 can bell peppers, diced
1 (8 ounce) can mushroom stems
    & pieces
2 cans Chinese mixed vegetables

1 can bamboo shoots
1 can water chestnuts
2 tablespoons soy sauce
salt and pepper to taste
3 to 4 packages won ton skins
oil for frying

Brown meat, drain grease and set aside. Scramble eggs, green peppers and mushrooms together. In a bowl, combine vegetables, bamboo shoots, water chestnuts, soy sauce, salt and pepper. Mix well. Combine all the ingredients together and mix well. Place 1 teaspoon of mixture on each won ton skin. Seal with water. Make up all egg rolls and lay out on wax paper before frying. Deep fry in hot oil and drain on paper towels.

"Great for a party when you need a lot of finger foods."

Janet Worland   **Silver Valley High School, Yermo, CA**

BABY PIZZAS

Serves 48 to 50

1 pound ground beef
1 pound hot Italian sausage
1 pound Velveeta cheese

1 (8 ounce) can tomato sauce
2 loaves party rye bread

Cook and drain ground beef and Italian sausage. Chop or grind cooked meats into fine pieces. Place in pan, add cheese and tomato sauce and heat until cheese has melted. Stir well. Spoon mixture on top of bread pieces and broil until brown and bubbly.
Note: These can be frozen in a single layer on a cookie sheet and cooked from a frozen state.

"These are always the most popular item at our Open House! As my mom (Maurine Griffenhagen) said: 'These are such a hearty appetizer -- men especially love them.' Thanks Mom!"

Gaylen Roe   **Magnolia Junior High School, Chino, CA**

SPINACH POM POMS

Makes approximately 65 hors d'oeuvres

2 (10 oz.) packages frozen chopped
    spinach
2 cups packaged herb-seasoned
    stuffing mix, crushed

1 cup grated parmesan cheese
dash nutmeg
6 eggs, beaten
3/4 cup butter, softened

Thaw spinach. Drain; squeeze out all excess moisture. Place in a medium bowl and blend in remaining ingredients. Shape into balls the size of walnuts. Refrigerate or freeze. Before serving, preheat oven to 350 degrees. Lightly grease baking sheets. Place chilled or frozen balls on baking sheets. Bake 10 to 15 minutes or until hot. Drain on paper towels. Serve with wooden picks and SPICY MUSTARD SAUCE, if desired.

SPICY MUSTARD SAUCE

Makes 1⅓ cups

⅓ to ½ cup dry mustard
½ cup white vinegar

½ cup sugar
1 egg yolk

Combine dry mustard and vinegar in small bowl. Cover and let stand at room temperature overnight. In a small sauce pan, combine mustard-vinegar mixture, sugar and egg yolk. Simmer over low heat until slightly thickened. Cover and store in refrigerator up to one month. Serve at room temperature.

Sheryal Walther   **Lakewood High School, Lakewood, CA**

CONFETTI BREAD

Serves 8 to 10

8 ounces cream cheese, softened
1 medium-sized pizza bread (such as Boboli)
1 package dry ranch dressing dip
1 green bell pepper
1 red bell pepper

1 yellow bell pepper
1 spear broccoli
1 carrot
1 small can chopped olives
optional: choice of other vegetables

Combine cream cheese and dip mix. Spread over pizza bread. Dice all vegetables and toss together. Spread tossed vegetables over cream cheese mixture and press in. Chill 1 hour. Cut into squares and serve.

"This festive looking appetizer is great to throw together to bring or have at a New Year's gathering."

LaRae Harguess   **Hesperia High School, Hesperia, CA**

QUICK MIX PEPPERONI BATTER BREAD

Makes 1 loaf

3¼ cups flour
2 tablespoons sugar
1 teaspoon salt
1 package Fleishmann's rapid rise yeast

½ cup pepperoni, finely chopped
2 tablespoons margarine, softened
1¼ cups hot water

Set aside 1 cup of flour. Mix remaining flour and other dry ingredients, including yeast in a large bowl. Stir pepperoni, margarine, and water into dry mixture. Mix in only enough reserved flour to make a very thick batter. Cover and let rest 10 minutes. Turn batter into a greased 1½ quart casserole. Cover and let rise in warm, draft-free place until doubled in size, about 30 to 45 minutes. Bake at 375 degrees for 35 minutes or until done. Remove from casserole; cool on a wire rack.

"One-half cup of coarsely grated sharp Cheddar cheese can be substituted for the pepperoni."

Jill Burnham   **Bloomington High School, Bloomington, CA**

NAVY BEAN SOUP

Serves 6 to 8

1 pound dry navy beans, soaked
  overnight
2 quarts water
1 pound meaty hambone
1 teaspoon salt
1 cup onion, chopped

1 bay leaf
3 sprigs celery leaves
6 whole peppercorns
¼ cup catsup
1 carrot, chopped

Soak dry beans in water overnight, drain. In morning, put all ingredients in a crock pot and cook on low for 10 to 12 hours or on high for 6 to 7 hours. Remove bone, leaf, peppercorns, and celery sprigs before serving. Taste for salt. Trim meat off hambone and return to soup.

"I make this great soup with the "Honey-Baked" ham hambone that we have left over from Christmas dinner. Great served with cornbread."

Adriana Molinaro   **Helix High School, La Mesa, CA**

SEAFOOD CHOWDER

1 tablespoon butter
1 large carrot, sliced
½ cup onion, minced
1 celery rib, sliced
3 potatoes, peeled and chopped
1 quart chicken stock
2 (6½ ounce) cans chopped clams,
  (reserve liquid)
1 teaspoon salt

¼ teaspoon white pepper
1 tomato, skinned, seeded and
  chopped
¼ cup zucchini, chopped
¼ cup cornstarch, dissolved in ½ cup
  cold water
½ cup heavy cream
½ pound scallops

Melt butter in a large saucepan or a stockpot. Saute carrot, onion, celery and potato about 6 to 8 minutes. Add chicken broth, juice from canned clams, salt and pepper. Bring to a boil; reduce heat and simmer about 15 minutes or until vegetables are tender. Add tomato and zucchini. Stir in cornstarch dissolved in cold water. Heat and stir until thickened. Just before serving, stir in cream, chopped clams and scallops. Heat through until scallops are done. Do not boil or overcook at this point or fish will toughen.

"My family's favorite! Add extra scallops and chowder can become a hearty main dish."

Judy Stinton   **Mt. Miguel High School, Spring Valley, CA**

BLACK-EYED PEA SALAD

Serves 4 to 6

1 can black-eyed peas, drained
1 can kidney beans, drained
1 cup celery, diced
1 bunch green pepper, chopped

1 small red onion, minced
1 red or green pepper, chopped (or half of each)
Lite Italian dressing

Mix all salad ingredients together in a bowl. Add dressing to taste and stir well. Cover and chill well.

"Some people believe that eating "black-eyed peas" on New Year's Day brings good luck! Enjoy!"

Judi Topp   **A. B. Miller High School, Fontana, CA**

CHILI

Serves 4

1 pound ground beef
½ cup onion, chopped
1 clove garlic, minced
2 to 3 teaspoons chili powder
dash cumin
1 teaspoon salt
1 (16 ounce) can tomato sauce

1 (1 pound) can pinto beans
Garnish:
chopped onion
chopped parsley
grated Cheddar cheese
dollops of sour cream

Crumble ground beef in skillet (casserole if microwave). Add onion and garlic. Cook, uncovered, until meat loses its red color (5 minutes in microwave). Add remaining ingredients. Cook ½ hour on range (or 10 minutes in microwave), covered. Stir occasionally. When ready to serve, garnish as desired.

"For more years than I care to remember, I have served this along with cornbread and honey to various visiting fans of the Rose Parade on New Year's Day."

Ellie Wildermuth   **La Canada High School, La Canada, CA**

New Year's

MR. JONES VEGETABLE QUICHE

Serves 8

1 cup shredded Swiss cheese or
   Monterey jack cheese
1 pie crust - prepared and unbaked
1½ to 2 cups vegetables, shredded
   (green pepper, carrots, zuchinni,
   onions, etc.)

3 eggs, beaten
1 cup nonfat milk, or evaporated milk
   or cream
¼ cup parmesan cheese

Place the grated cheese on the bottom of pie crust. Place the shredded vegetables on top of cheese. Beat the eggs and milk together and place on top of the vegetables. Sprinkle ¼ cup parmesan cheese on top. Bake at 350 degrees for 35 to 40 minutes until the center is firm. May be served warm or at room temperature.

"Dick Jones, the art teacher at Ball Junior High, gave me this delicious recipe. Thanks!"

Marianne Traw　　　　　　**Ball Junior High School, Anaheim, CA**

SEKIHAN (RED BEAN RICE)

Serves 6 to 8

¼ cup azuki (red beans)
3 cups mochigome (sweet rice)

1 tablespoon black sesame seeds
1 tablespoon salt

Wash azuki, drain water, then add 2 cups water. Bring to a boil and boil for 1 minute. Drain water. Add 2 cups fresh water and boil over low heat until beans are medium soft. Drain beans, reserving liquid. Place a wet cloth over the beans and refrigerate. Wash mochigome (sweet rice) and soak in the reserved liquid from the beans, overnight. Drain rice, reserve liquid. Mix the rice and beans together. Place in a steamer and steam for 40 to 50 minutes until rice is cooked. Baste with reserved liquid every 15 minutes. Toast the sesame seeds and mix with salt. Sprinkle the sesame seed salt mixture over the steamed red rice and serve hot.

"We serve this for happy occasions. The sekihan can be frozen, then microwaved to reheat."

Reiko Ikkanda　　　**South Pasadena Middle School, South Pasadena, CA**

CHICKEN SCALLOPINI WITH LEMON-THYME SAUCE

Serves 4

2 whole chicken breasts, boned,
   skinned and split
1 tablespoon butter or margarine
1 tablespoon salad oil
⅔ cup dry white wine (or regular
   strength chicken broth)

½ cup whipping cream
2 teaspoons lemon juice
½ teaspoon thyme leaves
salt and pepper to taste
parsley and lemon wedges for garnish

Place chicken breasts between sheets of plastic wrap or waxed paper and pound with a heavy wooden mallet evenly and gently until breasts are ¼" thick. Dust chicken with flour and shake off excess. In a wide frying pan, over medium-high heat, place butter or margarine and salad oil and melt. When melted, add as many chicken breasts as will fit without crowding and cook quickly about 1½ minutes per side or until meat loses its pinkness when slashed. Place on a hot platter and keep warm. Cook remaining pieces, adding more butter and oil as needed. Add to platter and keep warm. Add wine or chicken broth to browned particles in pan and boil until reduced by about half, stirring to blend. Add whipping cream, lemon juice and thyme leaves. Boil until sauce thickens slightly. Pour any meat juices that collect on serving platter into the sauce. Salt and pepper to taste. Pour over meat and garnish with parsley and lemon wedges.

"An easy and elegant dish!"

Shirley Wilcox   **Burbank High School, Burbank, CA**

3 BEAN CASSEROLE

Serves 10 to 12

½ pound bacon, cut up	*1 (15 oz.) can kidney beans*
½ pound ground beef	*½ cup catsup*
1 small onion, chopped	*½ to ¾ cup brown sugar*
2 (1 lb. 12 oz.) cans pork and beans	*1 heaping teaspoon mustard*
1 (15 oz.) can butter beans	*2 teaspoons vinegar*

Brown bacon and beef. Mix remaining ingredients together and add to meat mixture. Cook in a slow cooker for 1 ½ hours at high setting or in the oven at 350 degrees for ½ hour.

Susan Rohm   **Cimarron High School, Las Vegas, NV**

KENTUCKY BOURBON BALLS

Makes 5 dozen

⅛ pound butter (not margarine)	*1 (8 ounce) package unsweetened*
1 pound powdered sugar	*chocolate squares*
⅓ cup Kentucky bourbon	*2 tablespoons butter*
¼ pound pecans	*2 tablespoons paraffin*

Mix ⅛ pound butter and powdered sugar together until it looks like cornmeal. Add bourbon and mix with hands until smooth. Refrigerate at least 3 hours. Take out of refrigerator and roll walnut size dough around half of a pecan. Place in refrigerator overnight. Place chocolate, butter and paraffin in a double boiler over boiling water. After melting, turn heat down to low. Dip bourbon balls in chocolate mixture and place on waxed paper. When cool and set, store in airtight container.

"One of the advantages of coming from a Kentucky background."

Marilyn Tam   **Orange Glen High School, Escondido, CA**

INDIVIDUAL BAKED ALASKAS

Serves 4

3 egg whites
1/4 teaspoon cream of tartar
6 tablespoons sugar
1/2 teaspoon vanilla

1 package of 4 sponge cake dessert
  shells
1 pint ice cream, any flavor that
  is colored

Preheat oven to 500 degrees. Beat together the egg whites and cream of tartar until foamy. Add the sugar, two tablespoons at a time, while beating. Add vanilla and continue beating until stiff peaks form. Place dessert shells on an ungreased baking sheet and spoon the ice cream on top. Cover each one completely with the meringue, sealing to bottom. Bake for 3 to 4 minutes, or until light brown and serve immediately. The Baked Alaskas may be completely prepared ahead of serving time and fozen (let meringue freeze, then wrap). Bake as directed above when ready to serve.

"These are impressive to serve, but very rich."

Barbara Hansen   **Montclair High School, Montclair, CA**

ENGLISH TEA CAKES

Makes about 18

1 1/4 cups flour
1 1/2 teaspoons baking soda
1/4 teaspoon salt
3/4 cup sugar

1/2 cup butter or margarine, softened
1 egg
1 tablespoon milk
1/2 cup raisins or currants

Mix flour, baking soda and salt together. In a separate bowl, cream sugar, butter or margarine, and egg. Add dry ingredients, milk and raisins to creamed mixture just until blended. Grease or spray with vegetable spray baking tins for "tarts." (Tart tins are available in specialty kitchen shops and make these tea cakes in the shape of little flying saucers. It is also okay to fill muffin tins 1/3 full.) Pour batter into tins and bake at 325 degrees for 12 to 15 minutes.

"These are a simple, inexpensive and traditional little English treat. My mother got the recipe from her mother -- they are great with hot tea or coffee."

Susan Pearson   **Lincoln High School, Stockton, CA**

CHOCOLATE MOUSSE PIE

Serves 8

1 (8 squares) package Baker's
  semi-sweet chocolate
1/4 cup water

8 eggs, separated
1 1/2 teaspoons vanilla
2/3 cup sugar

Heat chocolate with water in saucepan over very low heat (or in microwave), stirring until smooth. Stir in egg yolks; add vanilla. Beat egg whites in a large bowl until foamy throughout. Gradually beat in sugar until stiff peaks form (about 3 minutes). Stir a small amount into chocolate mixture to lighten. Fold chocolate mixture into remaining egg whites. Pour 4 cups into a buttered 9" pie pan sprinkled with sugar. Chill remaining mixture. Bake at 350 degrees for 25 minutes or until just set. Cool slightly; then chill 1 hour. Center will fall forming a shell. Spoon chilled chocolate mixture into chilled shell. Chill 3 hours or overnight. Garnish with whipped cream and chocolate curls.

"This is an elegant but 'simple to make' dessert that is excellent for any holiday occasion! Any 'chocoholic' will love it!"

Ginger Russo   **Chico Junior High School, Chico, CA**

DUCK SAUCE (Chinese Chutney)

Makes 3½ cups

2 cups unsweetened applesauce
3 cups brown sugar
1 cup white vinegar
1 cup onion, chopped
2 cloves garlic, crushed

2 tablespoons ginger root, finely
  chopped
1 tablespoon dark soy sauce
1 teaspoon salt
¼ teaspoon red pepper flakes
1 tablespoon light mustard seed

Measure all ingredients into a 2 quart saucepan. Turn heat to high and bring to a rapid boil. Turn heat to medium and cook gently, stirring often. When it is the consistency of honey, remove from heat and transfer to sterile glass jars; seal. When cool, store in refrigerator.

"I make this for presents during the holiday! My friends love it. I usually double or triple the recipe to make enough."

Jeri Lundy   **Grossmont High School, La Mesa, CA**

VALENTINE'S DAY

SHRIMP SPREAD

Serves 6-8

4 small shallots (green onions)
1 cup mayonnaise
1 pound cooked shrimp
2 tablespoons capers

salt and pepper
paprika
rye melba toast

Mince shallots and mix with mayonnaise. Coarsely chop chrimp and add to mayonnaise mixture. Add capers and mix well. Add salt and pepper to taste. Put in a serving bowl, sprinkle with paprika. Serve with heated rounds of rye melba toast.

"Elegant appetizer to serve with a romantic Valentine's Day dinner."

Alice Lewandowski   **Linden High School, Linden, CA**

BREAKFAST CASSEROLE

Serves 6

1½ pounds sausage
6 eggs
6 slices white bread, torn
1 cup Cheddar cheese, grated
½ pound fresh mushrooms, sliced

1 (4 ounce) can Ortega chilies, diced
1 teaspoon salt
1 teaspoon dry mustard
2 cups milk

Mix all ingredients. Cover and refrigerate overnight. Turn into buttered 9"x13" pan. Bake for 30 minutes, covered, at 350 degrees. Remove cover and continue to bake for 30 minutes more.

Kathleen Yonter   **Burkholder Middle School, Henderson, NV**

SICILIAN SKILLET CHICKEN

Serves 4

4 boneless chicken breast halves
2 tablespoons Parmesan cheese, grated
3 tablespoons flour
salt and pepper to taste
2 tablespoons olive oil

1 cup mushrooms, sliced
½ onion, finely chopped
½ teaspoon rosemary, crushed
1 (14½ ounce) can Del Monte
  Italian style stewed tomatoes

Flatten chicken slightly. Coat with 4 tablespoons cheese, then flour. Salt and pepper to taste. In a skillet, cook chicken in oil over medium to high heat until done. Remove to serving dish. Keep warm. In the same skillet, cook mushrooms, onion and rosemary until soft. Add tomatoes; cook, uncovered, over medium to high heat until thickened. Spoon over chicken; top with remaining cheese. Serve over pasta.

"It's fast, easy and a nutritious meal."

Virginia Panttaja   **Sanger High School, Sanger, CA**

PORK WITH RASPBERRY VINEGAR SAUCE

Serves 4

4 boneless pork chops
2 tablespoons flour
salt to taste
1/4 teaspoons white pepper
1/2 teaspoon dried rosemary
1 cloves garlic, pressed

2 tablespoons oil
1/2 cup beef stock
1/2 cup vermouth
1/4 cup raspberry vinegar
1/4 cup heavy cream

Dredge pork in flour. Season with salt, pepper and rosemary. Sauté the garlic in the oil for 1 minute. Add pork and brown. Pour off fat in pan. Stir in beef stock and vermouth. Cover and simmer 20 to 30 minutes. Remove pork from pan and keep warm. Turn up heat to high and reduce sauce in pan until thick. Add vinegar and continue cooking until thickened. Add cream and simmer until thick enough to coat pork. Arrange pork on plates. Spoon over sauce. Serve immediately.

"Special meal for a special someone."

Julie Shelburne   **Tulare Union High School, Tulare, CA**

ELEGANT DIPPED STRAWBERRIES

Makes 18

1 (8 ounce) container non-fat plain
   yogurt
1/3 cup NutraSweet Spoonful
1 tablespoon skim milk
1/4 teaspoon orange rind, grated

1/4 teaspoon vanilla extract
18 large strawberries, with leaves
   intact, chilled
1/4 cup semi-sweet chocolate chips,
   melted

Line a colander or sieve with 2 layers damp cheesecloth or paper coffee filters and place in a large bowl. Stir yogurt until smooth. Pour yogurt into lined colander to drain. Refrigerate 24 hours. Place the resulting yogurt cheese in a bowl, discard cheesecloth and liquid.

Add NutraSweet Spoonful, milk, orange rind, and vanilla to yogurt cheese; mix well. Hold each strawberry by the leaves and dip into yogurt cheese to almost cover. Place on waxed paper-lined tray and chill. Drizzle chocolate over chilled strawberries. Store, uncovered, in refrigerator until ready to serve.

"This is a NutraSweet recipe that is wonderful! Everyone who has tried these strawberries has loved them!"

Patti Ligon   **Granite Hills High School, El Cajon, CA**

BLACK FOREST CHOCOLATE CHEESECAKE

Serves 12   **Photo on Cover**

COCOA CRUMB CRUST (recipe follows)
2 (8 oz. each) packages cream cheese,
   softened
1 (8 oz.) cup dairy sour cream
1¼ cups sugar
½ cup Hershey's Cocoa or Premium
   European Style Cocoa

3 eggs
2 teaspoons almond extract
WHIPPED CREAM TOPPING
   (recipe follows)
1 (21 oz.) can cherry pie filling, chilled

Heat oven to 350 degrees. Prepare COCOA CRUMB CRUST; set aside. In large mixer bowl, beat cream cheese, sour cream and sugar until smooth. Add cocoa, eggs and almond extract; beat just until blended. Pour over prepared crust. Bake 45 to 50 minutes or until center is almost set; remove from oven to wire rack. Cool 30 minutes. With knife, loosen cake from side of pan. Cool completely; remove side of pan. Cover; refrigerate. Just before serving, spread or pipe WHIPPED CREAM TOPPING around top edge of cheesecake; fill top with cherry pie filling. Cover; refrigerate leftovers.

COCOA CRUMB CRUST: In small bowl, stir together 1¼ cups graham cracker crumbs, ¼ cup Hershey's Cocoa or Premium European Style Cocoa, ¼ cup sugar and ½ cup (1 stick) melted butter or margarine. Press mixture firmly onto bottom of 9-inch springform pan.

WHIPPED CREAM TOPPING: In small mixer bowl, beat 1 cup (½ pt.) cold whipping cream, ¼ cup powdered sugar, and ½ teaspoon almond extract. Beat until stiff.

Hershey Foods Corporation   **Hershey, Pennsylvania**

BEST CHOCOLATE CHERRY MINI CAKES

Makes about 1½ dozen   **Photo on Cover**

1½ cups all-purpose flour
1 cup sugar
¼ cup Hershey's Cocoa or Premium
   European Style Cocoa
1 teaspoon baking soda
½ teaspoon salt

1 cup water
⅔ cup vegetable oil
1 tablespoon white vinegar
1 teaspoon vanilla extract
CHERRY CREAM FROSTING
   (recipe follows)

Heat oven to 350 degrees. Paper-line 18 muffin cups (2½ inches in diameter). In large mixer bowl, stir together flour, sugar, cocoa, baking soda and salt. Add water, oil, vinegar and vanilla; beat thoroughly. Fill each muffin cup ⅔ full with batter. Bake 15 to 20 minutes or until wooden pick inserted in center comes out clean. Cool completely. Prepare CHERRY CREAM FROSTING; pipe or spread onto top of each cupcake. Top with maraschino cherry. Cover; refrigerate leftovers.

Hershey Foods Corporation   **Hershey, Pennsylvania**

CHERRY CREAM FROSTING

¼ cup milk
2 tablespoons all-purpose flour
¼ cup shortening
1 teaspoon almond extract

2¼ cups powdered sugar
¼ cup maraschino cherries, chopped
and drained (optional)
Few drops red food coloring (optional)

In small saucepan, stir together milk and flour. Cook over low heat, stirring constantly with wire whisk, until mixture thickens and just begins to boil. Remove from heat; refrigerate until chilled. In small mixer bowl, beat flour mixture, shortening, almond extract and powdered sugar until smooth. If cherries are desired, dry thoroughly on paper towels; stir into mixture with food coloring, if desired.

Hershey Foods Corporation　　　　　　**Hershey, Pennsylvania**

FUDGY VALENTINE CAKE

Serves 10-12　　　　　　　　　　　　　　**Photo on Page 93**

⅔ cup butter or margarine, softened
1¾ cups sugar
2 eggs
1 teaspoon vanilla extract
1¾ cups all-purpose flour
¾ cup Hershey's Cocoa or Premium
European Style Cocoa

1½ teaspoons baking soda
1 teaspoon salt
1½ cups dairy sour cream
PINK BUTTERCREAM FROSTING
(recipe follows)
Chocolate curls (optional)

Heat oven to 350 degrees. Grease and flour two 9-inch heart-shaped pans.* In large mixer bowl, beat butter and sugar until light and fluffy. Add eggs and vanilla; beat well. Combine flour, cocoa, baking soda and salt; add to butter mixture alternately with sour cream, blending well. Beat 3 minutes on medium speed. Pour into prepared pans. Bake 35 to 40 minutes or until wooden pick inserted in center comes out clean. Cool 10 minutes; remove from pans to wire racks. Cool completely. Prepare PINK BUTTERCREAM FROSTING. Frost top of one layer; place second layer on top. Frost top and sides of entire cake. Garnish with chocolate curls, if desired.

Hershey Foods Corporation　　　　　　**Hershey, Pennsylvania**

PINK BUTTERCREAM FROSTING

½ cup butter or margarine, softened
4¼ cups powdered sugar
4 to 5 tablespoons milk

2 teaspoons vanilla extract
¼ teaspoon red food coloring

In small mixer bowl, beat butter untiil light and fluffy. Gradually add powdered sugar, alternately, with milk and vanilla until smooth and of desired consistency; stir in food coloring.

*NOTE: One 8-inch square baking pan and one 8-inch round baking pan (each must be at least 1½ inches deep) may be substituted for heart-shaped pans. Prepare, bake and cool cake as directed above. Cut round layer in half, forming 2 half circles; place cut edges against two adjoining sides of square layer to form heart. Frost entire cake.

Hershey Foods Corporation　　　　　　**Hershey, Pennsylvania**

MINIATURE CHOCOLATE CHEESECAKES

Photo on Page 93

1 (8 ounce) package cream cheese,
    softened
²/₃ cup sugar
¼ cup Hershey's Cocoa or Premium
    European Style Cocoa
1 tablespoon all-purpose flour
1 egg

½ cup dairy sour cream
½ teaspoon almond extract
9 single serve graham crusts
Whipped topping
VANILLA CHIP HEARTS or CHOCOLATE
    CHIP HEARTS (recipes follow)

Heat oven to 350 degrees. In small mixer bowl, beat cream cheese and sugar; blend in cocoa and flour. Add egg; blend in sour cream and almond extract. On cookie sheet, place crusts; fill each crust with cream cheese mixture to ¼-inch from top. Bake 15 to 20 minutes or just until center is almost set. Cool completely; cover and refrigerate. Just before serving, garnish with whipped topping and VANILLA CHIP HEARTS or CHOCOLATE CHIP HEARTS. Refrigerate leftovers. 9 cheesecakes.

VANILLA CHIP HEARTS: In medium microwave-safe bowl, place 1²/₃ cups (10 oz. pkg.) Hershey's Vanilla Milk Chips and 1 tablespoon shortening. Microwave at HIGH (100%) 1 minute; stir vigorously until chips are melted and mixture is smooth. On wax paper-covered tray, spread into rectangle, about 10x7-inches. Refrigerate until mixture just begins to set, about 10 minutes; cut into hearts with cookie cutters or knife. Cover and refrigerate; carefully remove from wax paper. About 18 hearts (2" wide).

CHOCOLATE CHIP HEARTS: In medium microwave-safe bowl, place 2 cups (12 oz. pkg.) Hershey's Semi-Sweet Chocolate Chips and 1 tablespoon shortening. Microwave at HIGH (100%) 1 to 2 minutes, or until chips are melted and mixture is smooth when stirred. Spread, cut and store as directed above.

Hershey Foods Corporation   **Hershey, Pennsylvania**

SWEETHEART STRAWBERRY CAKE

Serves 8 to 10

1 white cake mix
1 box strawberry gelatin
½ cup water
¾ cup salad oil
4 eggs
1 (8 ounce) package frozen
    strawberries, thawed and drained
    (reserving juice)

Frosting:
2 tablespoons margarine, softened
3 cups sifted powdered sugar
1 (8 ounce) package frozen
    strawberries, thawed and
    drained (reserving juice)

In a large bowl, combine white cake mix, gelatin, water, oil and eggs and beat on slow for 2 minutes; beat on high for 4 minutes. Stir in drained strawberries. Pour in a greased and floured 9"x13" pan. Bake at 350 degrees for 45 to 55 minutes. When cake is baked, while still warm, poke holes with toothpicks over ¼ of cake at a time. Spoon strawberry juice (reserved from 2 packages strawberries) into these holes. For frosting, beat margarine and powdered sugar together until creamy. Fold in the remaining package of strawberries. Frost cake when cooled, writing "I Love You" on top. (You may also use strawberries folded into a prepared can of buttercream frosting.)

Mary Richmond   San Luis Obispo High School, San Luis Obispo, CA

RED VELVET CAKE

Serves 16-20

½ cup margarine or butter	*1 teaspoon salt*
2 eggs	*1 cup buttermilk*
1½ cups sugar	*1 teaspoon vinegar*
2 tablespoons cocoa	*1 teaspoon baking soda*
1 to 2 ounces red food coloring	*1 teaspoon vanilla*
2½ cups cake flour	

Cream together margarine or butter, eggs and sugar. Make a paste of cocoa and part of food coloring. Add this and rest of food coloring to creamed mixture. Sift flour and salt. Add sifted flour alternately with buttermilk to creamed mixture. Add vinegar. Stir in soda and vanilla together, add to batter. Mix well. Bake in two 8" round cake pans (heart shaped if for Valentine's). Bake for 30 minutes at 350 degrees.

FROSTING:

1 cup margarine or butter	*3 tablespoons flour*
1 cup sugar	*1 tablespoon vanilla*
1 cup milk	

Cream butter and sugar until fluffy, with beater. Cook milk and flour until it thickens. Cool milk mixture, add vanilla to sugar and margarine, then add milk GRADUALLY, beating constantly. Do not frost sides. Keep refrigerated.

"Beautiful--worth the effort! A special taste treat for the holidays!"

Jean L. Dempsey   Santa Paula High School, Santa Paula, CA

SUGAR COOKIES

Makes about 2 dozen

½ cup butter or margarine	*2½ cups flour*
1 cup granulated sugar	*1 teaspoon baking powder*
2 eggs	
1 teaspoon vanilla (or other flavored extract)	

In a large bowl, cream together butter or margarine and sugar. Add eggs and vanilla; mix thoroughly. Stir in flour and baking powder. Wrap dough in wax paper and seal in an airtight container or "zipper" plastic bag. Refrigerate for 2 to 3 hours. Roll dough out on well-floured counter to ¼-inch thickness. Cut out desired shapes and bake on ungreased cookie sheet at 375 degrees for 5 to 7 minutes.

"This dough is very soft and can be re-rolled several times without becoming tough. The cookies are soft, not crispy. The students like to frost them with a buttercream frosting."

Cindy Peters   **Park Junior High School, Antioch, CA**

CHOCOLATE CHERRY FUDGE

Makes about 4 dozen   **Photo on Page 92**

⅓ cup maraschino cherries, well
*   drained and finely chopped*
½ cup butter
3⅔ cups powdered sugar
½ cup Hershey's Cocoa or Premium
*   European Style Cocoa*

¼ cup evaporated milk
⅓ cup pecan pieces
1 teaspoon almond extract
maraschino cherry halves, well
*   drained (optional)*
slivered almonds (optional)

Line 8-inch square pan with foil. Blot chopped cherries between layers of paper towels; set aside. In medium microwave-safe bowl, microwave butter at HIGH (100%) 1 minute or until melted; stir in powdered sugar, cocoa and evaporated milk until well blended. Microwave at HIGH 1½ minutes; stir vigorously. Microwave at HIGH an additional 30 seconds at a time, until mixture is hot, slightly thickened and smooth when stirred; do NOT boil. Stir in reserved chopped cherries, pecans and almond extract. Spread in prepared pan. Cover; refrigerate until firm. Remove foil; cut into squares. Garnish with maraschino cherry halves and slivered almonds pressed lightly onto fudge, if desired. Serve cold; refrigerate leftovers.

Hershey Foods Corporation   **Hershey, Pennsylvania**

CHERRY VANILLA CHIP BROWNIES

Makes about 16 brownies   **Photo on Page 92**

½ cup maraschino cherries, well
*   drained and chopped*
⅓ cup butter or margarine, softened
¾ cup sugar
2 eggs
2 tablespoons light corn syrup
1 tablespoon Kirsch (cherry flavored
*   liqueur)**
⅔ cup all-purpose flour
⅓ cup Hershey's Cocoa or Premium
*   European Style Cocoa*

¼ teaspoon baking powder
⅓ cup slivered almonds, chopped
1 cup vanilla milk flavored chips
VANILLA CHIP DRIZZLE (recipe follows,
*   optional)*
maraschino cherry halves, well
*   drained (optional)*

Heat oven to 350 degrees. Line 9" square baking pan with foil; grease and flour foil. Blot cherries between layers of paper towels; set aside. In small mixer bowl, beat butter, sugar, eggs, corn syrup and Kirsch until blended. Add flour, cocoa and baking powder; blend until combined. Stir in chopped cherries, almonds and vanilla chips. Pour into prepared pan; bake 25 to 30 minutes or until brownies begin to pull away from sides of pan. Cool completely in pan; cover and refrigerate until firm. Remove from pan; remove foil. Cut into shapes with cookie cutters, or cut into squares. Garnish with VANILLA CHIP DRIZZLE and maraschino cherry halves, if desired. Refrigerate until drizzle is firm; refrigerate leftovers.

VANILLA CHIP DRIZZLE: In small microwave-safe bowl, place ⅔ cup Hershey's Vanilla Milk Chips and 1 teaspoon shortening. Microwave at High (100%) 30 seconds; stir. If necessary, microwave at HIGH additional 15 seconds until chips are melted when stirred. Using tines of fork, drizzle across brownies.

*Or substitute 1 teaspoon almond extract plus 1 teaspoon vanilla extract for Kirsch.

Hershey Foods Corporation   **Hershey, Pennsylvania**

CHOCOLATE BUTTERCREAM CHERRY CANDIES

Makes about 4 dozen   **Photo on Page 92**

About 48 maraschino cherries with   *½ teaspoon vanilla extract*
*   stems, well drained*   *¼ teaspoon almond extract*
¼ cup butter, softened   *VANILLA CHIP COATING (recipe*
2 cups powdered sugar   *   follows)*
¼ cup Hershey's Cocoa or Premium   *CHOCOLATE CHIP DRIZZLE (recipe*
*   European Style Cocoa*   *   follows)*
1 to 2 tablespoons milk, divided

Cover tray with wax paper; blot cherries between layers of paper towels. In small mixer bowl, beat butter, powdered sugar, cocoa and 1 tablespoon milk until smooth; stir in vanilla and almond extract. If necessary, add remaining milk, a teaspoonful at a time, until mixture will hold together but is not wet. Mold scant teaspoonful mixture around each cherry, covering completely; place on prepared tray. Cover; refrigerate until firm, at least 3 hours. Prepare VANILLA CHIP COATING; holding by stem, dip each cherry into coating. Place back on tray; refrigerate until firm. About 1 hour before serving, prepare CHOCOLATE CHIP DRIZZLE; with tines of fork, drizzle randomly over candies. Refrigerate until drizzle is firm; refrigerate leftovers.

VANILLA CHIP COATING: In small microwave-safe bowl, place 1⅔ cups (10 oz. pkg.) Hershey's Vanilla Milk Chips; drizzle with 2 tablespoons vegetable oil. Microwave at HIGH (100%) 1 minute; stir vigorously until chips are melted and mixture is smooth. If necessary, microwave at HIGH additional 15 seconds; stir vigorously until smooth. If mixture thickens while coating, microwave at HIGH for 15 seconds; stir until smooth.

CHOCOLATE CHIP DRIZZLE: In small microwave-safe bowl, place ¼ cup Hershey's Semi-Sweet Chocolate Chips and ¼ teaspoon shortening. Microwave at HIGH (100%) 30 seconds to 1 minute; stir until chips are melted and mixture is smooth.

Hershey Foods Corporation   **Hershey, Pennsylvania**

MISSISSIPPI FUDGE

Serves 18 to 24

1 cup butter or margarine
1/3 cup cocoa
2 cups sugar
4 eggs
pinch salt
1 1/2 cups flour
1 1/2 cup walnuts, chopped

1 jar marshmallow cream
Frosting:
1/2 stick butter or margarine
1/3 cup cocoa
1 box powdered sugar
1/3 cup milk
1 tablespoon vanilla

Cream together butter, cocoa and sugar. Beat in eggs, one at a time. Add salt, flour and walnuts. Place mixture in a 9"x13" pan and bake at 350 degrees for 30 minutes. (DO NOT OVERBAKE!) Spread marshmallow cream over top and return to oven for 5 minutes. Remove from oven and allow to cool. Cream together ingredients for frosting; butter, cocoa, powdered sugar, milk and vanilla. Frost cake and cut into squares.

"This recipe is a chocolate lover's dream!"

Myra Skidmore   **Downey High School, Downey, CA**

CHOCOLATE COVERED CHERRIES

Makes 36 to 48 cookies

1/2 cup butter, softened
1 cup sugar
1 egg
1 1/2 teaspoons vanilla
1 1/2 cups flour
1/2 cup unsweetened cocoa
1/4 teaspoon salt
1/4 teaspoon baking powder

1/4 teaspoon baking soda
36 to 48 maraschino cherries, well
    drained (reserve 1 teaspoon juice)
Frosting:
1 cup semi-sweet chocolate pieces
1/2 cup sweetened condensed milk
1/2 teaspoon salt
1 teaspoon cherry juice

In a large mixing bowl, cream butter, sugar, egg and vanilla until light and fluffy. Add remaining ingredients and mix until a dough forms, about 1 minute. Shape into 1-inch balls, using a heaping teaspoon of dough for each. Push one cherry halfway into each ball.

Prepare frosting by melting ingredients in microwave until bubbly. Mix until smooth, and spoon over each cookie-covered cherry. Bake frosted cookies in a preheated 350-degree oven for 8 to 10 minutes, until puffy.

Carrie Drewisch   **Vandenberg Middle School, Lompoc, CA**

ST. PATRICK'S DAY

GREEN SLUSH BUCKET PUNCH

Serves 24

1 (12 ounce) can concentrated frozen
   lime punch
2 (12 ounce) cans concentrated frozen
   lemonade or pineapple juice

72 ounces (6 cans) water
1 gallon lime sherbet ice cream
1 (2 liter) bottle carbonated
   lemon-lime soda

Mix together frozen juices and water in a large plastic container or "bucket." Freeze overnight. Place in refrigerator 2 to 3 hours before serving. When ready to serve, place in a large punch bowl. Chop up into a slush consistency with a large spoon. Add and mix in the sherbet ice cream and pour in carbonated lemon-lime soda. Stir and ladle into cups immediately for a "slushy" taste.

"This is a thick punch with a tangy lemon-lime flavor."

Karen Thornton   **CerroVilla Middle School, Villa Park, CA**

ZUCCHINI & APPLE SALAD

Serves 8

$^1/_3$ cup salad oil
1 tablespoon lemon juice
2 tablespoons white wine vinegar
1 teaspoon sugar
1 teaspoon dry basil
$^3/_4$ teaspoon salt
$^1/_4$ teaspoon pepper

3 medium-sized red or golden
   delicious apples
$^1/_2$ medium red onion, thinly sliced
   lengthwise
1 green pepper, seeded and cut into
   matchstick pieces
1 pound zucchini, thinly sliced

In a large salad bowl, combine oil, lemon juice, vinegar, sugar, basil, salt and pepper. Core and dice unpeeled apples and add to dressing; coat apples well with dressing. Add onion, green pepper and zucchini. Stir lightly. Cover and chill.
Just before serving, mix salad again until well combined. Taste and add more salt if needed.

"This is a surprisingly delightful, unique combination of ingredients. It's a clean, crisp change of pace."

Lynda Waugh   **San Marcos Junior High, San Marcos, CA**

EMERALD RICE

Serves 6

4 eggs, separated
4 cups cooked rice
1 cup raw spinach, minced
$^1/_2$ cup green pepper, minced
$^1/_4$ cup onion, minced
1 cup heavy cream, whipped

$^1/_3$ cup grated Parmesan cheese
1 teaspoon paprika
1 teaspoon salt
1 cup sour cream
3 tablespoons chives, minced

Beat egg yolks. Add rice, spinach, green pepper, onion, cream, cheese, paprika, and salt. Fold in stiffly beaten egg whites. Pour into ring mold; set in a pan of water and bake at 350 degrees for 45 minutes. Garnish with sour cream and chives.

"It's fun to do an all-green-foods St. Patrick's Day party--amazing varieties of green foods exist."

Jeanne Limmer   **Los Alamitos High School, Los Alamitos, CA**

MOM'S IRISH CHEESECAKE

Makes 1 cheesecake

Graham Cracker Crust:
¼ *cup sugar*
¼ *cup butter or margarine, melted*
1 package graham crackers, crushed
Filling:
16 ounces cream cheese, softened
¾ *cup sugar*
2 eggs, beaten

2 teaspoons lemon juice
2 to 10 drops green food coloring
Topping:
1 cup sour cream
3 tablespoons sugar
1 teaspoon vanilla
2 to 10 drops green food coloring

Prepare crust: thoroughly mix sugar, butter or margarine and graham cracker crumbs and press into an 8" to 9" round cake pan, reserving 1 tablespoon of mixture. Bake at 350 degrees for 15 minutes, or until brown. Cool.

Prepare filling: beat cream cheese until smooth. Add remaining ingredients and beat until frothy, adding food coloring until desired shade of green is acquired. Pour into cooled crust and bake at 350 degrees for 15 to 20 minutes.

Prepare topping: mix ingredients well and pour over cooked filling. Sprinkle with one tablespoon of graham cracker mix. Bake 5 minutes more at 350 degrees. Cool 3 to 5 hours before serving (the longer the better--overnight is great).

"Creative people can even attempt to draw a shamrock in the center of the cheesecake."

Julie Carriere   **No. Monterey County High School, Castroville, CA**

PISTACHIO CAKE

Serves 12 to 15

1 box white cake mix
1 box pistachio instant pudding
4 eggs

1 cup vegetable oil
1 cup ginger ale
1 cup walnuts, chopped

Beat all ingredients together for two minutes. Pour into a well-greased bundt pan. Bake at 350 degrees for 45 to 50 minutes. Cool in pan for 10 minutes, then turn out on serving plate. When thoroughly cooled, frost and enjoy.

Frosting:
8 ounces Cool Whip

1 box pistachio instant pudding
½ *cup milk*

Fudgy Valentine Cake, Page 84 & Mini Chocolate Cheesecakes, Page 85

Chocolate Cherry Fudge, Page 87, Cherry Vanilla Brownies, Page 87,
Chocolate Buttercream Cherry Candies, Page 88

Easter Bonnet Cookies, Page 103, Marzipan Easter Eggs, Page 104,
and Coconut Nests, Page 105

Beat all ingredients together until smooth and creamy. May be made ahead of time and refrigerated.

"This recipe is so easy and really delicious."

Joanne Fial   **East Middle School, Downey, CA**

BLARNEY STONES

Makes a lot!

Cake:
4 eggs, separated
2 cups sugar
1 cup boiling water
2 cups flour
1 tablespoon baking powder
1 teaspoon vanilla

Icing:
1 pound Crisco (approximately
  2¼ cups)
½ pound butter or margarine
3 pounds powdered sugar
milk
1 teaspoon vanilla
2 pounds peanuts, ground

Lightly grease two 9"x13" pans or two jelly roll pans. Preheat oven to 375 degrees. Beat egg yolks with sugar until creamy. Add boiling water. Sift together flour and baking powder. Add to creamed mixture. Add vanilla. Beat egg whites until stiff. Fold into flour mixture. Turn into baking pans and bake 25 to 30 minutes. Cool and cut into 1" squares.

For icing: cream together shortening and butter or margarine. Add powdered sugar slowly. Add just enough milk to make icing spreading consistency. Beat in vanilla. Ice each square, then roll in ground peanuts. Keep in an airtight container. These also freeze well.

"Mom always makes these for St. Patrick's Day. They are delicious--you cannot eat just one."

Maria Fregulia   **Lassen Union High School, Susanville, CA**

MINT CHOCOLATE COOKIES

Makes 6-7 dozen

¾ cup margarine
1½ cup brown sugar
2 teaspoons water
1 (12 oz.) package semi-sweet
  chocolate chips

2 eggs
2½ cups flour
1¼ teaspoons baking soda
½ teaspoon salt
1 box Andes Mints

Melt margarine in a saucepan over medium heat. Add sugar, water and chocolate chips and blend well with a wooden spoon. Remove from heat and beat in eggs.

Stir dry ingredients together in a large electric mixing bowl. Pour chocolate mixture into flour and beat until well blended. Cover bowl and chill two hours.

Mold 1-inch balls and place 2 inches apart on a foil-lined cookie sheet. Bake at 350 degrees for 8 to 10 minutes (tops should crack).

Unwrap and break mints in half. Remove foil with cookies onto countertop and put half an Andes mint on top of each cookie. Spread to frost when mint has softened.

Patty Dyle   **John F. Kennedy High School, La Palma, CA**

GRASSHOPPER PARFAITS

Serves 4

1 package vanilla pudding mix   *1 tablespoon creme de cacao*
2 tablespoons green creme de menthe   *½ cup chocolate wafer crumbs*

Mix the pudding according to package directions. Fold in creme de menthe and creme de cacao. Chill for 30 minutes. Layer the pudding and the crumbs in parfait glasses using about 1 tablespoon crumbs between layers. Chill.

Judy Hevener   **Porterville High School, Porterville, CA**

"DIG IN" CAKE

Serves 12

8 ounces cream cheese   *1 large box instant vanilla pudding*
1 stick margarine   *12 ounces Cool Whip*
1 cup powdered sugar   *1¼ pound Oreo cookies*
3 cups milk   *gummy worms*

Mix together cream cheese, margarine and powdered sugar in one bowl. This is mixture #1.

Mix together the milk and pudding according to package directions. Fold in Cool Whip. This is mixture #2.

For dirt...crush Oreos in ziplock bag and roll with a rolling pin. This is mixture #3.

Layer mixture in a plastic 8" flower pot. Start with mixture #3, then mixtures #1, #2 and #3, ending with mixture #3 on top. Chill 4 hours. Add gummy worms and plastic floral centerpiece according to holiday (poinsettias for Christmas, daffodils for Easter, clover for St. Patrick's Day, etc.).

"Serve it up using a spade and place mixture into small flower pots (plastic works best to clean up!)."

Jill Sweet Anderson   **Santa Paula High School, Santa Paula, CA**

EASTER

ALMOST PINK CHAMPAGNE

Serves 20 (½ cup servings)

1 (25.4 ounce) bottle sparkling white grape juice
1 (25.4 ounce) bottle sparkling pink grape juice

1 (28 ounce) bottle club soda
1 tablespoon lemon juice

In a large non-metal pitcher or punch bowl, combine all ingredients; stir to blend and serve immediately.

"A great non-alcoholic punch."

Laura May　　　　　　　　**Hesperia Junior High School, Hesperia, CA**

EASTER EGGS

Serves 4 to 6

4-6 hard boiled eggs, chopped
1 package Schilling Cheese Sauce Mix

4 to 6 English muffins, split and toasted

Make cheese sauce according to package directions. Add chopped eggs and blend. Pour mixture over buttered muffins and serve.

"This recipe is also good with scrambled eggs. I made this up about 22 years ago to use up leftover Easter eggs."

Jane Van Wagoner　　　　　　　　**Walnut High School, Walnut, CA**

EASTER BRAID

Serves 10 to 12

½ cup milk
1 envelope active dry yeast
⅓ cup sugar
4 tablespoons butter, melted and cooled
2 eggs + 1 egg yolk
1 teaspoon salt
¼ teaspoon ground cinnamon
3 to 3½ cups flour
½ cup golden raisins

¼ cup slivered, blanched almonds
5 hard-cooked eggs, tinted in pastel colors
1 egg white, lightly beaten
Confectioner's Sugar Icing
1 cup sifted (10 times) confectioner's sugar
1 teaspoon lemon juice
3 to 4 teaspoons boiling water

Heat milk in a small saucepan over low heat until very warm. Sprinkle yeast and 1 teaspoon of the sugar into the milk; stir to dissolve. Let stand to proof until bubbly, about 10 minutes. Combine remaining sugar, butter, eggs and yolk, salt and cinnamon in a large bowl. Stir in yeast mixture. Beat in 3 cups of the flour, 1 cup at a time, until mixture forms a soft dough. Turn dough out onto a lightly floured surface and knead 8 minutes or until smooth and elastic, using as much of the remaining flour as necessary to prevent dough from sticking. Press dough into a large buttered bowl; turn to bring buttered side up; cover. Let rise in a warm place away from draft, 1½ hours or until doubled. Punch dough down. Turn out onto a lightly floured surface and knead in raisins and almonds. Divide dough in half; roll dough between palms of hands into two ropes, 26 inches long. Place ropes diagonally on an ungreased cookie sheet. Braid ropes starting in center, working toward each end and placing tinted eggs between the ropes after each twist. Gently curve the braid into a circle; place a generously greased 5 ounce heat-proof glass dish in the center of the circle to keep braid in a neat round. Finish braiding the ropes, pinching the ends securely together; cover. Let rise in a warm place about 1 hour or until doubled in volume. Brush dough with egg white. Bake in a moderate oven (350 degrees) for 25 minutes. Gently remove glass from center. Bake 10 minutes longer or until bread is golden brown and sounds hollow when tapped lightly with finger tips. Cool on wire rack. Drizzle with Confectioner's Sugar Icing.

To make icing: Blend sugar and lemon juice in a small bowl. Gradually add enough water to make icing thin enough to drizzle.

Note: For frozen bread dough Easter Braid, add 1 teaspoon grated orange rind to icing.

"These make great Easter gifts for friends and family."

Cindy Bowman   Mc Farland High School, Mc Farland, CA

PORTUGUESE SWEET BREAD

Serves 10

1 package dry yeast	*¼ cup butter*
¼ cup warm water	*3 eggs*
½ cup milk	*1 teaspoon grated lemon peel*
⅔ cup sugar	*3½ to 4 cups unsifted flour*
¼ teaspoon salt	*1 egg white*

Place yeast and warm water in mixing bowl for 5 minutes. Scald milk; let cool. Add milk, sugar, butter, eggs, and lemon peel. Mix thoroughly. Add flour, one cup at a time, until a soft dough forms and leaves the sides of the bowl. Turn out on floured surface. Knead for 8 minutes. Let rise for 2 hours. Shape dough into a flat 9 inch round. Let rise for 1½ hours. Brush with egg white. Bake in 350 degree oven for 45 to 50 minutes. Let cool. Serve.

Betty Wells   Oroville High School, Oroville, CA

ALMOND-LIME LOAF

Makes 1 loaf

3 cups flour, sifted	*1 egg*
1 cup sugar (for batter)	*1 cup milk*
3 teaspoons baking powder	*5 tablespoons butter or margarine,*
1 teaspoon salt	*melted*
¼ teaspoon baking soda	*3 tablespoons lime juice*
1 (3 oz.) package sliced almonds	*2 tablespoons sugar (for topping)*
2 tablespoons grated lime rind	

Grease a 9" x 5" x 3" loaf pan. Sift together flour, the 1 cup sugar, baking powder, salt and soda into a large bowl; stir in ¾ cup of the almonds and 1 tablespoon lime rind. Beat egg well with milk in a small bowl; stir in 4 tablespoons of the melted butter and 2 tablespoons of the lime juice. Add all at once to flour mixture. Stir just until evenly moist. Spoon into prepared pan; spread top to make even. Combine remaining almonds and 1 tablespoon melted butter with the 2 tablespoons sugar in a cup; spoon evenly over batter. Bake at 350 degrees for one hour and 10 minutes, or until a wooden pick inserted in the center comes out clean. Cool in pan on a wire rack for 10 minutes. Loosen around edges with a knife; turn out onto rack, place right side up. Drizzle remaining 1 tablespoon lime juice over loaf, then sprinkle remaining 1 tablespoon lime rind on top. Cool completely. Wrap loaf in waxed paper, foil or plastic wrap. Store overnight to mellow flavors. Slice thinly to serve.

Linda Robinson   **Royal High School, Simi Valley, CA**

POPOVERS

Makes 10 to 12

4 eggs	*1 teaspoon salt*
1½ cups milk	*¼ cup butter, melted*
1½ cups flour	

Preheat oven to 400 degrees. Grease well, a popover pan (or muffin tins). Mix all ingredients in a blender and pour into cups until they are ⅔ full. Bake for 40 minutes. Serve hot.

"These are great stuffed with butter and your favorite jam. We always had these with sausages for Christmas or Easter breakfasts."

Carrie Drewisch   **Vandenberg Middle School, Lompoc, CA**

PINEAPPLE-ORANGE DELIGHT

Serves 15

1 can Mandarin oranges	*1 teaspoon vanilla*
1 (15 ounce) can crushed pineapple	*4 tablespoons powdered sugar*
1 (3 ounce) package tapioca pudding	*4 cups whipping cream*
1 (3 ounce) package lemon pudding	*1 package Knox Unflavored Gelatin*
3 cups hot water	*¼ cup water*
1 (3 ounce) package orange Jello	

Drain oranges and pineapple. Set aside. (Pineapple juice may be used as a part of the water.) Add tapioca pudding and lemon pudding to water. Brind to a boil. Remove from heat and add dry orange Jello. Stir until dissolved. Cool. Add vanilla and powdered sugar to whipping cream. Soften unflavored gelatin in ¼ cup water; heat until dissolved. Whip cream and when it begins to thicken, slowly pour in gelatin. Continue beating until stiff. Fold pudding mixture into whipping cream mixture. Fold fruit into cream mixture. Pour into mold or 9" x 13" pan. Chill until set.

"Great recipe to take to a party or dinner, may be used as a salad or dessert as needed."

Mary Lash **Paramount High School, Paramount, CA**

ORANGE ALMOND SALAD

Serves 4

1 head lettuce
1 cup celery, diced
1 small can Mandarin oranges
¼ cup slivered almonds
2 tablespoons sugar

Dressing:
2 tablespoons cider vinegar
¼ cup salad oil
dash of pepper
2 tablespoons sugar
½ teaspoon salt
¼ teaspoon almond extract

Prepare salad by combining lettuce, celery and oranges. In a saucepan, combine almonds and sugar. Stir until almonds are coated and lightly browned. Cool and break apart. Add to salad. Prepare dressing by combining ingredients and pouring over salad just before serving.

"Any salad ingredient can be used. The important part is the slivered almonds and the salad dressing."

Marie Coots **Huntington Beach High School, Huntington Beach**

SEAFOOD COLESLAW SALAD

Serves 16+

1 head cabbage, shredded
1 green onion, chopped
¼ head red cabbage, shredded

1 pound shrimp
½ pound imitation crab
1 bottle "Hidden Valley" ranch dressing

Toss all ingredients in a bowl, 24 hours in advance of serving to allow flavors to integrate.

"Delicious! Great, elegant salad for buffet or served as individual servings on a lettuce leaf. Top with paprika."

Nan M. Paul **Grant Middle School, Escondido, CA**

HOT CHICKEN SALAD

Serves 12

4 to 5 cups cooked chicken breasts,
    cut up
1 can cream soup (chicken, celery,
    or mushroom)
2 cups celery, cut up
4 tablespoons onion, minced

1 cup almonds (can be seasoned)
1 cup mayonnaise
½ teaspoon pepper
2 tablespoons lemon juice
1 cup cracker crumbs
6 hard cooked eggs, chopped

Toss all ingredients together and place in 1 large or 12 individual casseroles. Bake at 350 degrees for 30 minutes.

"Good way to use up hard cooked eggs. You can also substitute cut up turkey."

Kay Linberger   **Tokay High School, Lodi, CA**

SALMON CAKES

Serves 6

1 (15½ ounce) can salmon
½ cup green onions, chopped
¼ cup mayonnaise
2 tablespoons dry bread crumbs
2 tablespoons lemon juice
1 egg, beaten

¼ teaspoon oregano, crushed
¼ teaspoon cracked black pepper
2 tablespoons flour
1 tablespoon cornmeal
1 tablespoon margarine
1 tablespoon oil

Drain salmon, reserving 2 tablespoons liquid; flake. Combine salmon, green onions, mayonnaise, bread crumbs, reserved salmon liquid, lemon juice, egg and seasonings. Mix thoroughly. Cover and refrigerate at least 30 minutes. Combine flour and cornmeal. Melt butter in a skillet. Add oil. Make patties out of salmon mixture and coat each side of patty with flour-cornmeal mixture. Pan fry over medium to medium-high heat for 3 to 4 minutes per side or until golden brown.

"This is a great recipe for Lent."

Diane Castro   **Quartz Hill High School, Quartz Hill, CA**

HAPPY HOLIDAY HAM

Serves 10 to 12

6 (12 ounce) bottles stout beer
    (Guiness or Sierra Nevada brand)
smoked ham, boneless or bone-in
3 to 4 bay leaves

3 tablespoons Coleman's dry mustard
1 cup plum jam
pineapple circles

Boil ham in beer with bay leaves for 1½ to 2 hours, depending on size. Mix mustard and jam to make a glaze. Arrange pineapple circles on ham with toothpicks. Spread glaze over ham. Bake at 350 degrees for 1½ to 2 hours. Slice and serve.

"This is THE BEST recipe for holiday ham. The boiling tenderizes and flavors the ham while the baking dries it a little. It literally melts in your mouth -- and it's easy!"

Michael A. Rupp　　　　　　　　　**Live Oak High School, Live Oak, CA**

SHISH-KA-BOB

Serves 8-10

lamb or beef, cubed (3 to 4 pounds)	*2 tablespoons oil*
vegetables of your choice	*⅓ cup cooking sherry*
Marinade:	*½ teaspoon pepper*
1 clove garlic, minced	*½ teaspoon oregano*
1 medium onion, chopped	*1¼ teaspoons salt*

Remove all fat from meat and cut into cubes. Blend marinade ingredients and pour over meat. Refrigerate overnight. Arrange on skewers alternating with vegetables of your choice. (I use red and green pepper, cherry tomatoes, and onion.) Grill on barbeque. Great served with rice pilaf.

"This recipe was given to me by my aunt who is a great cook."

Peggy Himenes　　　　　　　**Actis Junior High School, Bakersfield, CA**

BROCCOLI CASSEROLE

Serves 8 to 10

Broccoli spears, fresh	*¼ cup mayonnaise*
1 can cream of mushroom soup	*2 tablespoons lemon juice*
½ cup sour cream	*Cheet-O cheese crackers, crumbled*

Combine soup, sour cream, mayonnaise and lemon juice. Lightly butter a 9" x 12" glass casserole. Parboil, steam or microwave broccoli just until tender. Arrange in casserole dish and spread soup mixture on top. Top with crumbled cheese crackers and bake at 325 degrees for 30 to 40 minutes.

"Everyone loves this at any holiday. Especially good with baked ham, roast beef and turkey. You can substitute frozen broccoli spears for fresh."

Libby Bruce　　　　　　　　　**Troy High School, Fullerton, CA**

SUNDAY GLAZED CARROTS

Serves 4

6 to 8 medium carrots, sliced	*2 tablespoons cold water*
2 tablespoons butter	*1½ teaspoons cornstarch*
¼ cup brown sugar, firmly packed	*¼ cup pecans, chopped*

Place carrots in a 1 quart casserole with butter and brown sugar. Cover and microwave on High for 9 minutes, stirring after 5 minutes. Mix water and cornstarch until smooth. Stir into carrot mixture. Add pecans and cover. Microwave on High 2 to 4 minutes until sauce has thickened. Stir before serving.

"Excellent! These candied carrots are perfect for a holiday meal or anytime special."

Karen Bennett   **Norco High School, Norco, CA**

CHEESY POTATOES

Serves 6 to 8

1 (32 ounce) bag frozen hashbrowned
  potatoes
1 can creamy chicken mushroom soup
  or cream of mushroom soup

½ pint sour cream
½ cup milk
1 cube margarine, melted
1 cup Cheddar cheese, grated

In a bowl, mix together hashbrowned potatoes with soup, sour cream and milk. When mixed well, add melted butter and about ½ of the grated cheese. Spread into a greased 9" x 13" pan and top with remaining cheese. Bake at 350 degrees, uncovered, for about 45 minutes.

"This serves as a great side dish for a ham dinner, or you can add diced ham and serve as a main dish.

Nancy Kappe   **Rancho Verde High School, Moreno Valley, CA**

SPINACH CASSEROLE

Serves 8

2 packages frozen chopped spinach
½ cup onion, chopped
¼ cup butter or margarine
¼ cup flour
1½ teaspoons salt

⅛ teaspoon pepper
2 cups milk
2 tablespoons lemon juice
6 eggs

Cook and drain spinach. In a saucepan, saute onion in butter and blend in flour, salt and pepper. Add milk and cook to form a white sauce. Remove from stove. Add spinach and lemon juice. Beat well. Add eggs and heat again. Pour into 1½ quart shallow casserole. Place in pan of hot water in oven and bake at 350 degrees for 40 minutes or until knife inserts and comes out clean. Serve with a cheese sauce.

"A good side dish with ham."

Jeanette Mitzenmacher   **Antelope Valley High School, Lancaster, CA**

STRAWBERRY WAFFLES

Serves approximately 8

4 eggs, separated
2 cups milk
2⅓ cups flour
¼ cup sugar

1 teaspoon salt
5 teaspoons baking powder
2 tablespoons margarine, melted

Separate eggs into two large bowls. Into egg yolks, add milk and mix well. Mix the dry ingredients together and add to the egg yolk and milk mixture. Beat egg whites until stiff peaks form. Fold into waffle batter. Gently add melted margarine. Bake in a waffle iron that's been seasoned and preheated. Top with vanilla ice cream.

"This has been an Easter Sunday favorite for many years -- the guests vary, but we always serve this."

Carol Buhman   Fountain Valley High School, Fountain Valley, CA

HOMEMADE VANILLA ICE CREAM

Makes 2 quarts

3 large eggs
1⅓ cups sugar
2 quarts Half & Half

2 tablespoons vanilla (my husband
likes one extra tablespoon!)

In a large electric mixer bowl, combine ingredients and mix well. Pour into an electric ice cream freezer and freeze, adding rock salt to ice in proportions to freeze. After about 30 minutes, put ice cream into tightly sealed containers in refrigerator-freezer. Let "age" at least 2 hours.

"Put on top of home baked waffles and top both with sliced, fresh strawberries."

Carol Buhman   Fountain Valley High School, Fountain Valley, CA

EASTER BONNET COOKIES

Makes about 2½ dozen   **Photo on Page 93**

1 cup Mazola margarine
⅔ cup sugar
½ cup Karo light corn syrup
1 tablespoon lemon juice

2 eggs
3½ cups unsifted flour
Decorator's Frosting (recipe follows)

In large bowl with mixer at medium speed, beat margarine, sugar, corn syrup, lemon juice and eggs until well blended. Gradually add flour; beat until well blended. Cover; refrigerate overnight. On lightly floured surface, roll out dough, ⅓ at a time, to ⅛-inch thickness. Cut with 3½-inch scalloped or plain edged round cookie cutter. Remove all excess dough and reserve for use later. Place rounds on ungreased cookie sheets. Bake in 350 degree oven 10 minutes or until lightly browned around edges. Remove and cool on wire racks. Using rounded teaspoons of reserved excess dough, shape into balls. Place on ungreased cookie sheets. Bake in 350 degree oven 10 to 12 minutes or until set and lightly browned on bottom. Remove and cool on wire racks. Prepare 2 separate batches of Decorator's Frosting. Spread small amount of frosting on bottom of each cookie ball and place in center of round cookie. Let stand until set. Color one batch of the frosting as desired using paste food colors. Stir in small amount of water until mixture flows from spoon in slow even stream. (Frosting should be the consistency of canned chocolate syrup.) Brush frosting over top of cookies leaving edges unfrosted. Let stand until set. Divide and color remaining frosting. Using pastry bag fitted with small decorator tips, pipe on ribbons and flowers. Let stand until set. Store in tightly covered containers.

Decorator's Frosting

Makes about 2 cups

In large bowl with mixer at low speed, beat 1 pound confectioners sugar, 3 egg whites and ½ teaspoon cream of tartar until blended. Beat at high speed 7 to 10 minutes or until knife drawn through mixture leaves a path. Before and while using, keep frosting covered with damp cloth.

Best Foods   **Englewood Cliffs, New Jersey**

MARZIPAN EASTER EGGS

Makes 12   **Photo on Page 93**

1 cup almond paste
¼ cup Karo light corn syrup
¼ cup Mazola margarine, softened
½ teaspoon almond extract

1 pound confectioners sugar
1 (6 oz.) package semisweet chocolate
  pieces
Decorator's Frosting (recipe follows)

In large bowl with mixer at medium speed, beat together almond paste, corn syrup, margarine and almond extract until well blended and smooth. Beat in about 1 cup of the confectioners sugar until well blended. With wooden spoon, stir in as much of the remaining confectioners sugar as possible. With hands, knead in any remaining confectioners sugar until marzipan is smooth and holds together. Divide into 12 equal pieces. Form each piece into an egg shape. Place on waxed paper-lined tray. Refrigerate several hours or until firm. In 1-quart saucepan, heat chocolate pieces over low heat until melted; stir until smooth. Dip each egg halfway into chocolate. Stand each egg upright on waxed paper-lined tray. Refrigerate until chocolate is set. Decorate as desired with Decorator's Frosting. Let stand until set. Store in tightly covered container in cool place.

Food Processor Method: Place almond paste, corn syrup, margarine and almond extract in work bowl of food processor with metal blade. Process until smooth and well blended. Add confectioners sugar, about ⅓ at a time; process until well blended after each addition. On surface lightly dusted with confectioners sugar, knead just until marzipan holds together.

Makes about 2 cups

In large bowl with mixer at low speed, beat 1 pound confectioners sugar, 3 egg whites and ½ teaspoon cream of tartar until blended. Beat at high speed 7 to 10 minutes or until knife drawn through mixture leaves a path. Divide frosting and tint as desired. Keep frosting covered with damp cloth.

Best Foods   **Englewood Cliffs, New Jersey**

COCONUT FONDANT NESTS

Makes about 2½ dozen   **Photo on Page 93**

1 pound confectioners sugar, sifted,
_   divided_
½ cup Karo light corn syrup
⅓ cup Mazola margarine
1 teaspoon vanilla

2 drops green food color
2 (4 oz. each) packages shredded
_   coconut_
tiny jelly beans (assorted colors)

In 3-quart saucepan, stir together 2 cups of the confectioners sugar, corn syrup and margarine. Stirring constantly, bring to full boil over medium-low heat. Stir in remaining sugar. Remove from heat; cool 5 minutes. Stir in vanilla and food color. With wooden spoon, beat until mixture thickens slightly. Stir in coconut just until blended. Drop by heaping teaspoonfuls into mounds onto waxed paper-lined tray. Press 3 jelly beans into each mound to form nest. Let stand until set. Store in tightly covered container.

Best Foods   **Englewood Cliffs, New Jersey**

CRISPY MALLOW EASTER NESTS

Serves 10 or 12

7 oz. jar marshmallow creme
¼ cup peanut butter
½ cup butterscotch chips

5 oz. can chow mein noodles
small jelly beans

Place first three ingredients in large glass bowl. Microwave 3 minutes at medium power. Stir until smooth, then add chow mein noodles, mixing until noodles are thoroughly coated. Drop noodle mixture by rounded tablespoonfuls onto greased cookie sheet; shape with greased fingers to form nests. Press 3 small jelly beans into center of each nest. Let stand until firm.

"This is a fun recipe for kids to do, and it's tasty too!"

Penny Niadna   **Golden West High School, Visalia, CA**

MILLION DOLLAR FUDGE

Makes 25 to 30 eggs

4¹/₂ cups sugar
2 tablespoons butter
¹/₄ teaspoon salt
1 (13 oz.) can evaporated milk

12 oz. semi-sweet chocolate chips
12 oz. german sweet chocolate (3 bars)
1 pint marshmallow creme
2 cups nuts, coarsely chopped

Boil first 4 ingredients for 6 minutes -- stirring constantly. Place remaining ingredients in a bowl. Pour boiling syrup over ingredients in bowl; beat until chocolate is all melted and pour into a 9" x 13" pan. Let stand a few hours before cutting. Store in a tin box.

For Easter Eggs: Use large spoon to scoop out amount for each egg and shape. Put on wax paper on cookie sheet. For coating, use any large chocolate bar or 12 ounces of melted chocolate chips. Use table knife to cover bottom, sides and top; put on cookie sheet in refrigerator to set fast. Wrap in plastic wrap and foil and tie with gift ribbon and silk flowers.

"Great Easter eggs for stuffing into baskets!"

Astrid Curfman   **Newcomb Middle School, Long Beach, CA**

KOLACKY

Makes 10 to 12 dozen

1¹/₂ cups margarine (do not use butter)
3 (3 ounces) packages cream cheese
3 cups flour

powdered sugar
canned filling or jam

Cream margarine and cream cheese thoroughly. Blend in flour and mix well. Roll into 12 balls. Cover with plastic wrap and refrigerate at least 6 hours or overnight. Preheat oven to 350 degrees. Lightly grease baking sheets. Liberally sprinkle working surface with powdered sugar. Place one ball of dough at a time (keep remainder refrigerated) on sugar and roll into 9" circle. Cut into about 9 wedges. Place 1 teaspoon filling at wide edge of wedge and roll into crescent shape. Bake 20 to 25 minutes or until bottoms of crescents are lightly browned. Remove from baking sheet immediately and cool. Sprinkle with powdered sugar. Store in airtight container.

"I love to take these to holiday potlucks because I always take home an empty plate. Experiment with different fillings. I especially like apricot, almond and poppyseed."

Kathy Warren   **C.K. McClatchy High School, Sacramento, CA**

CINCO DE MAYO

FESTIVE GAZPACHO

Serves 8 to 12

1 1/2 cloves garlic
3 teaspoons salt
1/2 cup mushrooms, chopped
4 tablespoons olive oil
1 1/2 cup green pepper, finely chopped
1 1/2 cup onion, finely chopped
1 1/2 cup celery, finely chopped
1 1/2 cup cucumber, finely chopped

3 cups tomatoes, chopped
3 teaspoons chives, chopped
2 tablespoons parsley, chopped
1 1/2 teaspoons freshly ground black
   pepper
1/2 to 1 teaspoon Tabasco sauce
1 1/2 teaspoons Worcestershire sauce
3/4 cup tarragon vinegar
4 to 5 cups tomato juice

Crush garlic in 1 teaspoon of the salt. Sauté mushrooms in olive oil until lightly browned. Combine mushrooms and garlic with remaining ingredients in a stainless steel or glass bowl. Cover and chill at least 4 hours or overnight. Serve with plain or garlic croutons, if desired.

"This is a perfect hot weather recipe--a real hit at a family barbecue or picnic."

Linda Paskins   **Cordova High School, Rancho Cordova, CA**

CHILI BEAN DIP

Makes 4 cups

1 (16 ounce) can refried beans
1 (4 ounce) can chopped green chiles

1/4 cup milk
1 pound light Velveeta cheese, cubed

Combine beans, chiles and milk. Add the cheese cubes. Stir over low heat until cheese melts. Serve hot with corn or tortilla chips.

"This is a fun way to teach 'legumes'."

Mary M. Rector   **Valley High School, Las Vegas, NV**

SALSA CRUDA

Serves 8

2 medium tomatoes, peeled
1/2 small onion
1 clove garlic

1 serrano chile
1/4 cup cilantro
1 teaspoon salt

Chop vegetables, add salt and mix well. Serve as an appetizer with chips or as an accompaniment with meat, beans or rice.

"This is an authentic salsa recipe brought back from the IMLE Cooking School I attended in Leon, Mexico."

Gail Hurt   **Estancia High School, Costa Mesa, CA**

GUACAMOLE

Serves 8

3 large avocados, peeled and chopped
½ small onion, chopped
1 medium tomato, chopped
2 small serrano chiles, chopped

1 tablespoon olive oil
1 teaspoon lemon juice
1 teaspoon salt

Mix all ingredients. If a smoother product is desired, prepare in a food processor and start with the chiles.

"I attended a cooking school in Leon, Mexico and brought back this authentic recipe. It's great!"

Gail Hurt **Estancia High School, Costa Mesa, CA**

FESTIVE MEXICAN DIP

Serves 10

1 cup cheese, shredded (diced Velveeta works well)
1 (32 ounce) can Dennison's chili con carne with beans

1 (6 ounce) can Ortega chiles, diced
2 packages corn chips

Mix cheese, Dennison's chili and Ortega chiles together. Heat in microwave oven on HIGH for 3 to 4 minutes or until it reaches desired temperature. Serve as a dip surrounded by corn chips.

"Easy, fast and delicious dip."

Rosemary Garland **Ontario High School, Ontario, CA**

TOSTADA DIP

Serves 10 to 15

5 avocados, peeled and mashed
guacamole dip mix
1 large can refried beans
16 ounces sour cream
1 (16 ounce) jar salsa
1 cup Ortega chiles

1 large square Monterey Jack cheese, grated
1 large square Cheddar cheese, grated
1 onion, chopped
1 can chopped olives
2 large tomatoes, chopped

Combine avocados and guacamole mix together. Set aside. On a large platter, spread beans on entire surface. Layer with sour cream, guacamole dip, salsa, chiles. Combine grated cheeses with onion and olives and layer on top of chiles. Top with chopped tomatoes.

"This is a great recipe for friends or large gatherings. Always comes out great!"

Linda Batchelor **Hesperia High School, Hesperia, CA**

SUPER NACHOS

Serves 10 to 12 as an appetizer; 4 to 6 as a main dish

1 pound lean ground beef
1 large onion, chopped
1 teaspoon Lawry's seasoned salt
½ teaspoon ground cumin
2 (1 pound) cans refried beans
1 (1¼ ounce) package Lawry's Taco
    Seasoning Mix (optional)
2 cups Monterey Jack cheese, grated

1 (4 ounce) chopped green chiles
1 cup Cheddar cheese, grated
¾ cup chunky taco sauce
tortilla chips
Garnishes:
1 cup sliced ripe olives
1 cup guacamole
½ cup sour cream
¼ cup green onion, chopped

Brown meat and onions in skillet; drain well and add seasoned salt and cumin. Combine beans, taco seasoning mix and Jack cheese; mix well. Spread beans in a shallow baking dish. Cover with meat mixture. Sprinkle chiles over meat, top with Cheddar cheese. Pour taco sauce over cheese. Bake, uncovered, in a 400-degree oven 20 to 25 minutes or until thoroughly heated. Tuck tortilla chips around edges of platter and garnish as suggested.

"This dish may be cooked in a microwave also. Heat for 10 minutes on HIGH, turning halfway through cooking. It also may be made the day before and refrigerated. Increase cooking time, heating until hot."

Eileen Jackson   **Lexington Junior High School, Cypress, CA**

CHILIQUILES

Serves 4 to 6

12 corn tortillas
1 cup red chili sauce
½ cup tomato sauce
½ teaspoon garlic salt

1½ cups Cheddar cheese, grated
1 green onion, chopped
2 tablespoons cilantro, chopped
oil for cooking

Tear tortillas into bite-size pieces. Fry until crisp and lightly browned. Drain grease from pan. Add chili sauce, tomato sauce, and garlic salt. Stir and cover until liquid is absorbed, on low heat. Add cheese, green onion and cilantro. Cover to melt cheese; serve at once.

Olga Sarouhan   **Edison High School, Huntington Beach, CA**

CHILE QUICHE

Serves 10-12

5 eggs
¼ cup flour
½ teaspoon baking powder
dash of salt
¼ cup butter, melted

1 (7 ounce) can diced green chiles
1 cup cottage cheese (small curd)
8 ounces shredded cheese (Jack and
    Cheddar mixed)

Beat eggs. Add dry ingredients, butter, chiles, cottage cheese and shredded cheese. Pour into a lightly greased 10" quiche dish or pie pan, or double the recipe and bake in a 9"x13" dish. Bake at 400 degrees for 15 minutes. Reduce the heat to 350 degrees and bake for 40 minutes more. Cut into 1-inch squares for cocktails.

Katherine Iverson   **Vandenberg Middle School, Lompoc, CA**

CHICKEN OR BEEF ENCHILADA CASSEROLE

Serves 10 to 12

*6 to 8 chicken breasts, cooked
   and chopped
   or
2 pounds ground round, browned
1 small onion, diced
2 to 3 garlic cloves, minced
1 (16 ounce) can olives, chopped*

*1 small can green chiles, chopped
   (no seeds)
1 (32 ounce) can red enchilada sauce
1 (16 ounce) can tomato sauce
1 dozen corn tortillas, chopped
2 cups Cheddar cheese, shredded
2 cups Monterey Jack cheese, shredded*

Cook meat, onion and garlic until done. If using the cooked chicken, sauté the onion and garlic until transparent; add the chicken, olives, chiles, enchilada sauce, and tomato sauce to make the filling. In a 9"x13" casserole dish, layer ½ chopped tortillas, ½ meat filling, ½ cheese. Repeat. Bake at 350 degrees for 45 minutes.

"Easy, tasty and feeds lots!"

Gail McAuley   **Lincoln High School, Stockton, CA**

CHILI RELLENO CASSEROLE

Serves 8

*2 (4 ounce) cans whole green chiles
8 ounces Monterey Jack cheese,
   shredded
8 ounces Cheddar cheese, shredded
2 eggs
2 tablespoons flour
1 can evaporated milk*

*Sauce:
2 cloves garlic, crushed
1 onion, sliced
1 green pepper, sliced
2 tablespoons oil
1 can beef bouillon
1 (8 ounce) can peeled tomatoes,
   chopped
1 teaspoon oregano
salt and pepper to taste*

Split chiles; discard seeds and rinse in cold water. In a 9"x13" pan, place layers of chiles and grated cheese; repeat layers until all is used. Beat eggs with flour and milk and pour over chiles and cheese. Bake, uncovered, at 350 degrees for 45 minutes. Serve with sauce.

For sauce: sauté garlic, onion and green pepper in oil. Add beef bouillon, tomatoes, oregano and salt and pepper to taste. Simmer for 30 minutes. Serve over baked casserole.

"Everyone raves about this casserole from my mother-in-law's collection."

Mary M. Rector   **Valley High School, Las Vegas, NV**

ESTHER'S TAMALE CASSEROLE

Serves 5-6

3 (28 ounce) cans tamales with gravy   1 cup Cheddar or Monterey Jack
2 cans cream of mushroom soup   cheese, grated
2-3 cups chicken, cooked and diced

Preheat oven to 350 degrees. Unwrap tamales and cut into chunks. Pour into a greased 9"x13" casserole dish. Mix tamale gravy with soup; set aside. Sprinkle diced chicken over tamales. Pour tamale gravy/soup mixture over tamales. Top with grated cheese. Bake for 20-30 minutes or until heated through.

"This winning recipe was given to me by my retired Home Economics friend, Esther Mayer."

Nanci Burkhart   **Hueneme High School, Oxnard, CA**

TORTILLA CASSEROLE

½ cup oil, for frying   garlic salt to taste
18 corn tortillas, cut into pieces   1 large onion, chopped
1 large can Chili de Las Palmas sauce,   Monterey Jack or Cheddar cheese,
    plus 1 can of water   grated (as desired)
1 (8 ounce) can tomato sauce   chopped olives (as desired)
salt to taste

Heat oil and fry a small amount of tortilla pieces at a time until golden brown. Set aside. In a large saucepan, put both sauces and 1 can of water (use Chili de Las Palmas can), salt, garlic salt and onion and cook for 10 minutes. In a large bowl, mix together tortilla pieces and sauce. Put mixture in a 9"x13" pan, garnish with grated cheese and olives as desired. Bake at 350 degrees for 20 to 30 minutes. NOTE: You can add cooked ground beef, chicken or turkey.

"My mother-in-law gave this recipe to me when I first got married. It's fast, easy and economical. It's great for Cinco de Mayo celebration or any time."

Tricia Montelongo   **South Junior High School, Anaheim, CA**

SOUR CREAM ENCHILADAS

Serves 4 to 6

2 cans cream of chicken soup
1 cup sour cream
1 (4 ounce) can diced green chiles
½ teaspoon salt
2 cups longhorn cheese, grated
½ cup green onions, chopped
1 (4 ounce) can chopped ripe olives,
    drained

1 pound hamburger, browned and
    drained
1 dozen corn tortillas
1 cup oil
1 cup sour cream

Combine soup, sour cream, chiles and salt in a saucepan and heat until smooth. Mix together cheese, onions, olives and hamburger. Dip tortillas in hot oil a few seconds, just to soften. Divide hamburger filling onto tortillas and roll each one. Place in 9"x13" pan; pour sauce over all and drop remaining sour cream by spoonfuls on top. Bake 30 minutes at 350 degrees.

"Whenever I take this to pot luck dinners, I know the pan will come home empty!"

Marianne Estes   **La Mirada High School, La Mirada, CA**

THE WHOLE ENCHILADA

Serves 8   **Photo on Page 124**
Preparation time: 15 minutes
Cooking time: 2 hours and 30 minutes to 3 hours

2½ pounds boneless beef chuck cross
    rib pot roast, cut into 8 pieces
1 tablespoon vegetable oil
½ cup onion, chopped
1 can (4 ounces) chopped green chiles
2 jalapeño peppers, seeded and finely
    chopped*
1 clove garlic, minced
½ cup single-strength beef broth
1½ teaspoons chili powder

½ teaspoon ground cumin
⅛ teaspoon each ground red pepper
    and salt
8 flour tortillas (6 to 7 inches)
1 (16 ounce) jar taco sauce
1 cup (4 ounces) Cheddar cheese,
    shredded
dairy sour cream or plain yogurt
green onion, finely chopped

Cut roast into 8 pieces. Heat oil in Dutch oven over medium-high heat until hot. Cook onion, green chiles, jalapeño peppers and garlic in hot oil 2 minutes, stirring frequently. Add beef chuck cross rib pot roast pieces and broth; sprinkle with chili powder, cumin, ground red pepper and salt. Reduce heat; cover and simmer 2 to 2½ hours or until beef is tender. Shred beef with two forks and mix well with pan juices.

Divide beef mixture evenly among tortillas; roll up. Spread small amount of taco sauce evenly over bottom of 11"x7" baking dish. Place tortillas, seam-side down, in dish; top evenly with remaining taco sauce. Sprinkle evenly with cheese. Bake in 375-degree (moderate) oven 15 minutes or until hot. Garnish with sour cream and green onion.

*For spicier beef mixture, do not remove the seeds from jalapeño peppers.

Nutrient data per serving for each enchilada: 407 calories, 13 g fat; 1,010 mg sodium; 100 mg cholesterol.

National Live Stock and Meat Board   **Chicago, IL**

CHICKEN ENCHILADAS WITH GUACAMOLE

Serves 8

2 cups cooked chicken, chopped	*guacamole*
1 medium onion, chopped	*sliced olives*
2 green chiles, chopped	*Guacamole:*
2 cups tomato puree	*2 ripe avocados*
1 dozen flour tortillas	*1 tablespoon chopped chiles*
oil for frying	*1 tomato, chopped*
6 chicken bouillon cubes	*1/4 cup onion, minced*
3 cups sweet warm cream	*1 tablespoon lemon juice or to taste*
1/2 pound Monterey Jack cheese, cubed	*salt and pepper to taste*

Mix chicken, onion, chiles and tomato puree. Fry tortillas in oil to soften. Dissolve bouillon in cream. Dip tortillas in cream mixture; fill with chicken and roll up. Place in a flat casserole dish, such as a 9"x13" one. Cover with remaining cream mixture. Sprinkle with Jack cheese. Bake at 375 degrees for 15 to 20 minutes or until heated through. Top with guacamole and sliced olives.

Mash avocados and add to other guacamole ingredients. Taste carefully for seasonings. Chill until ready to use.

"These are great and may be made with crab; either way, they are sensational!"

Helen Lievre   **La Canada High School, La Canada, CA**

MEXICAN STYLE CHICKEN

Serves 8

8 chicken breasts, skinned and boned	*1 tablespoon chili powder*
1 (7 ounce) can Ortega chiles, diced	*1/2 teaspoon salt*
4 ounces Monterey Jack cheese	*1/4 teaspoon cumin*
cut into 8 strips	*1/4 teaspoon pepper*
1/2 cup dry bread crumbs	*1/2 cup butter, melted*
1/4 cup Parmesan cheese	

Pound chicken to ¼-inch thickness. Inside chicken, place 2 tablespoons chiles and one piece of cheese. Roll chicken around chiles and cheese. Mix all dry ingredients in one bowl and melt butter in another bowl. Carefully dip chicken in butter and roll in dry ingredients. Place in 8"x16" pan. Chill at least four hours or overnight. Bake at 400 degrees for 20 minutes.

"If you're careful, you won't need toothpicks to hold these shut."

Pat Hufnagel　　　　　　　　　**Esperanza High School, Anaheim, CA**

THE BEST BOIL 'N ROAST CARNITAS

Serves 16 to 18

1 pork shoulder or butt, 5 to
*　5½ pounds*
3 large carrots, chopped
2 large onions, chopped
½ teaspoon each: ground coriander,
oregano leaves, chili powder, ground
*　cumin*

6 cups water
1 (12 ounce) jar green chili salsa
1 (7 ounce) can diced green chiles
½ cup green onions, thinly sliced
*　(including tops)*
16 to 18 warm corn or flour tortillas
*　(6-8" size)*

Place pork in a 6 to 8-quart pan; add carrots, onions, spices and water. Bring to a boil over high heat; reduce heat; cover and simmer until pork is very tender when pierced, 3 to 3½ hours. Lift meat from broth (reserve broth for soup or other uses, if desired) and place in a 9"x13" pan. Bake, uncovered, at 350 degrees until meat is well browned, 45 minutes to 1 hour. Drain off all fat, then shred meat, discarding bones and pieces of fat. (Makes about 8 cups.) Stir salsa, chiles and green onions into meat; return to oven until hot, 10 to 15 minutes.

To serve, spoon meat mixture into soft tortillas; roll to enclose and eat out of hand.

"The result is meat of unsurpassed tenderness and crispness, supported by a spicy (but not aggressive) green sauce."

Carol Goddard　　　　　　　　　**Alhambra High School, Alhambra, CA**

CHORIZO

Makes 1 pound

1 pound lean pork, coarsely ground
1 teaspoon salt
2 tablespoons chili powder

1 garlic clove, crushed
1 teaspoon oregano
2 tablespoons vinegar

Mix all ingredients thoroughly. Store in a glass or crockery container in refrigerator.

"My favorite use for chorizo is to brown and scramble with eggs and serve in a warm flour tortilla."

Bonnie Shrock　　　　　　　　　**Kearny High School, San Diego, CA**

CARNE ASADA

Serves 3 to 4

1 flank steak
1/4 cup chili powder
1/2 cup oil
1/3 cup lemon juice

1/2 teaspoon garlic powder
1/2 teaspoon salt
1/2 teaspoon MSG (optional)
1/2 teaspoon oregano

Tenderize the meat by pounding or cutting across the grain. Mix all other ingredients to make a marinade. Marinate the meat overnight. Grill on medium coals. Serve with warm tortillas, lettuce, tomatoes, onion, avocados and salsa.

"An inexpensive roast may be used (i.e. clod roast). Have your butcher cut into thin pieces. Be sure to marinate overnight."

Bonnie Shrock   **Kearny High School, San Diego, CA**

CHICKEN CHILE

Serves 6 to 8

1 whole chicken or 6 chicken breasts
1 cup onion, finely chopped
1 bell pepper, finely chopped
2 teaspoons garlic powder
1 teaspoon chili powder
3 teaspoons cumin

1 small can Ortega diced chiles
1/2 cup Pace Picante Sauce
2 cans (14 oz.) stewed diced tomatoes
1 can (14 oz.) tomato sauce
2 large cans pinto beans, drained

Cook chicken until well done. Debone and shred. Combine chicken and above ingredients in the order listed. Simmer for 45 minutes.

"This is a favorite of several of my friends. There are never any leftovers; add a green salad and bread, and dinner is complete!"

Karen Tilson   **Poly High School, Riverside, CA**

TACO SOUP

Serves 6 to 8

1 large onion
1 pound ground beef
salt to taste
1 package taco seasoning
1 large can tomatoes, with liquid
1 can corn, with liquid

1 can black olives, with liquid
1 can kidney beans, with liquid
sour cream
green onions, chopped
cheese, grated
taco chips

Sauté onion and ground beef; drain. Add salt to taste and taco seasoning. Add tomatoes, corn, olives, and kidney beans, all with liquid. Simmer 30 minutes. Serve with garnishes: sour cream, green onions, grated cheese and taco chips.

"Delicious soup to serve for a tree trimming evening or on Cinco de Mayo. Hot corn bread and a green salad complete the meal."

Alice Lewandowski   **Linden High School, Linden, CA**

IRMA'S SHRIMP SOUP

Serves 4 to 6

12 large tiger shrimp
2 stalks celery, diced
1 medium onion, diced
1 tomato, diced
2 small yellow chiles, seeded and diced
1 California chile, seeded and diced

1 tablespoon olive oil
salt to taste
garlic powder to taste
2 bouillon cubes
3 cups water

Clean shrimp and cut into thirds. In a 10-inch skillet, sauté celery, onion, tomato and chiles in olive oil for 3 to 5 minutes. Add shrimp and sauté until pink. Sprinkle salt and garlic powder over sautéed ingredients. Add bouillon cubes and water. Simmer 15 to 20 minutes. Serve hot.

"Great served with warm flour tortillas!"

Angela Croce   **Mira Mesa High School, San Diego, CA**

SOUTHWESTERN PASTA SALAD

Serves 4 to 6

4 cups pasta, cooked
1 red pepper, diced
1 avocado, diced
1/2 pound shrimp, cooked
Dressing:
2/3 cup mayonnaise

1/2 cup cilantro, chopped
2 tablespoons lime juice
1/2 teaspoon salt
dash of pepper
5 drops Tabasco sauce

Blend dressing ingredients together. Toss pasta with pepper, avocado, shrimp and dressing. Serve in a bowl garnished with lettuce and tomato.

"CRE winner."

Connie Halloway   **Fontana High School, Fontana, CA**

MEXICAN CHEESECAKE

Serves 18

6 eggs
1 1/8 cups sugar
3/4 cup margarine, melted
2 cups low-fat cottage cheese

2 cups light sour cream
2 tablespoons grated Parmesan cheese
1-1/ cups Bisquick

Beat eggs in a large mixing bowl until light and fluffy. Add sugar, margarine, cottage cheese, sour cream, Parmesan cheese and Bisquick. Mix well. Pour the mixture into a greased 9"x13" baking pan. Bake at 300 degrees for 30 minutes. Increase baking temperature to 325 degrees and bake an additional 30 minutes. Cool completely. Garnish with fruit slices or edible flowers. Refrigerate leftovers.
NOTE: Can be prepared one day ahead.

"Very light and tasty! People love it! Serve as an appetizer or dessert."

Ruth C. Gillmore   **Covina High School, Covina, CA**

AMERICA'S HOLIDAYS

Fourth of July

Labor Day

Mother's Day   Father's Day

COCOA MOCHA

Serves 12

1 can sweetened condensed milk
1 (4 ounce) bar German sweet
    chocolate

1 cup whipped cream

Melt chocolate with condensed milk over low heat. Cool. Fold in whipped cream. To serve: put about ¼ cup mixture into a mug. Fill to the top with coffee. Store remaining mix in refrigerator.

"I picked up this recipe from a cooking class. It's the BEST beverage dessert I've ever had!"

Linda Silvasy   **Olive Pierce Middle School, Ramona, CA**

FRESH FRUIT DIP

Makes approximately 2 cups

1 small package instant vanilla
    pudding mix
1 cup milk

rind of 1 orange
¼ cup orange juice
8 ounces sour cream (regular or lite)

Combine all ingredients, blend well. Store, covered, in refrigerator.
Serve with any fresh fruit cup for dipping.

"This is so easy and tasty, I've used it for lots of showers, buffets, barbeques...everyone asks for the recipe."

Lorna Wilfert   **Huntington Beach High School, Huntington Beach, CA**

AHWAHNEE CREAMED BANANAS

Serves 6

2 egg yolks
¼ cup sugar
1 teaspoon lemon juice
¼ teaspoon vanilla

1 (8 oz.) package cream cheese
1 tablespoon whipping cream
6 bananas
shaved chocolate

Beat together egg yolks, sugar, lemon juice and vanilla in a bowl. In a separate bowl, beat cream cheese and whipping cream. Blend into egg mixture. Slice bananas crosswise. Add to creamy mixture. Toss lightly to mix well. Sprinkle shaved chocolate over to garnish.

"A side dish served at breakfast buffets at the Ahwahnee Hotel, Yosemite."

Bonnie Pius   **Sanger High School, Sanger, CA**

BUBBLE BREAD

Serves 8

18 frozen "Bridgeford" Parker House
   rolls, thawed
½ package butterscotch pudding
   (not instant)

cinnamon
pecans, chopped
½ cup butter or margarine
½ cup brown sugar

Spray a bundt pan with "Pam". Place rolls in pan. Sprinkle with dry butterscotch pudding. Sprinkle with cinnamon, then nuts. Melt the butter or margarine with brown sugar and pour over top of rolls. Cover with waxed paper and a dish towel and allow to raise in warm place overnight. Bake for 30 minutes in a preheated 350 degree oven. Cool 15 to 20 minutes and turn out onto plate.

"The rolls are in the frozen food section of the store. This is delicious."

Carmen Leonard   Mission Viejo High School, Mission Viejo, CA

CHERRY CHEESE PASTRY

Serves 8 to 10

5 ounces cream cheese
⅓ cup sugar
2 teaspoons lemon juice
2 cups Bisquick

¼ cup butter
⅓ cup milk
1 can cherry pie filling

In a medium bowl, cream together cream cheese, sugar and lemon juice; set aside. In a large bowl, place Bisquick and butter, cutting in butter. Add milk and stir with a fork until a ball forms. Turn dough onto a floured surface and roll into a 10" x 16" rectangle. Spread filling down center ⅓ of the dough (lengthwise). Cut dough into 1 inch wide strips on both sides of filling; fold strips in criss- cross fashion over filling. Slide onto an ungreased baking sheet. Bake at 425 degrees 15 to 20 minutes, or until lightly browned. After baking, spread pie filling down center.
Note: Best if served at room temperature or refrigerated.

"Students love this one: It looks so impressive, just the thing to make for Mom on her special day."

Carol Wolff   Desert Springs Middle School, Desert Hot Springs, CA

RAISIN BRAN MUFFINS

Makes 2½ dozen

1 cup all bran cereal
1 cup raisins
1 cup boiling water
½ cup vegetable oil
1 cup sugar (can use ½ brown sugar,
   ½ white sugar)
¼ cup honey
2 cups buttermilk, room temperature

2 eggs, beaten
1½ teaspoon vanilla
2 tablespoons molasses
2 teaspoons orange peel
2½ cups flour
1 tablespoon baking soda
1 teaspoon salt
2 cups all bran cereal, crushed

Combine 1 cup all bran cereal, raisins and boiling water; set aside. Mix together oil, sugar, honey, buttermilk, eggs, vanilla, molasses and orange peel. Combine with bran mixture. Mix together flour, baking soda and salt. Add to bran mixture, stirring until flour mixture just disappears. Fold in crushed bran cereal into muffin batter. Refrigerate over night. Use paper muffin cup liners or grease (spray with Pam) muffin tins and fill cups ½ full with batter. Bake for 25 minutes at 350 degrees.

Note: Batter keeps covered in refrigerator for 10 days.

"This is a super recipe! The muffins are moist and just about everyone loves them. The best part is, the batter keeps well, is done ahead, so you can have no-muss, no-fuss, fresh muffins for meals. The baked muffins also freeze well."

Ellen Black-Eacker   **Nogales High School, La Puente, CA**

MOM IDA'S DANISH ABLESKIVER OR PANCAKES

Serves 4

3 cups "Bisquick"
½ cup sour cream
1 teaspoon baking soda
1½ cups milk
1 teaspoon lemon extract

¼ teaspoon nutmeg
3 egg yolks, lightly beaten
3 egg whites, stiffly beaten
salad oil

Combine Bisquick, sour cream, and baking soda in a bowl. Slowly add milk, lemon extract, nutmeg, and the egg yolks. Beat until smooth. Fold in egg whites. Put about 1½ teaspoons oil in each hole in the ableskiver pan. After oil is hot, pour in batter to fill hole. Fry until golden brown.

Note: This recipe also makes wonderful pancakes.

"Ida Troutman was my friend's Danish grandmother. This is one of the recipes that she converted from her Danish homeland."

Judy Conner   **Santa Ana Valley High School, Santa Ana, CA**

FRENCH BREAKFAST PUFFS

Serves 12

5 tablespoons plus 1 teaspoon
*   shortening*
½ cup sugar
1 egg
1½ cups flour
1½ teaspoons baking powder
½ teaspoon salt

¼ teaspoon nutmeg
½ cup milk
for dipping and rolling:
½ cup margarine, melted
1 teaspoon cinnamon
½ cup sugar

Cream together shortening, ½ cup sugar and egg. Sift together flour, baking powder, salt and nutmeg. Stir dry ingredients into creamed mixture alternately with milk. Pour into a greased muffin tin (12 muffin cups) and bake at 350 degrees for 20 minutes. Remove from oven and immediately dip puffs in melted butter, then roll in cinnamon/sugar mixture. Serve warm.

"This was my favorite recipe when I was in Home Economics at Downey High School, 25 years ago, and so I use it in my classes now."

Paula Skrifvars   **Brea Junior High School, Brea, CA**

ORANGE-LIME JELLO

Serves 10

1 (3 ounce) package orange Jello   *1 cup crushed pineapple*
1 package miniature marshmallows   *¼ pint whipped cream*
½ cup mayonnaise   *1 (6 ounce) package lime Jello*
1 (3 ounce) package cream cheese   *¼ cup nuts, chopped (optional)*

Add liquid to orange Jello, according to package directions. Melt marshmallows in Jello (stir together in saucepan). Let cool and gel slightly. Mix mayonnaise, cream cheese, crushed pineapple and whipped cream with orange Jello mixture. Let set in a 9" x 13" pan. Mix lime Jello according to package directions. Let cool slightly. Pour lime Jello onto orange mixture. Sprinkle with nuts and chill.

"A favorite at our family gathering for years. Change lime Jello to another color (such as red) for the different holidays."

Karen Lopez   **San Luis Obispo High School, San Luis Obispo, CA**

SPINACH SALAD

Serves 6

1½ pounds fresh spinach, washed and   *¼ cup cider vinegar*
*   trimmed*   *¼ cup sugar*
8 fresh mushrooms, sliced   *½ teaspoon salt*
8 slices bacon, cooked and crumbled   *½ teaspoon paprika*
3 eggs, hard-cooked   *¼ teaspoon dry mustard*
1 large avocado, ripe   *coarsley ground fresh black pepper*
Dressing: *¼ medium white onion, finely*
½ cup olive oil   *   chopped*

Toss all salad ingredients together and set aside. Combine dressing ingredients in a jar and shake thoroughly. Refrigerate until ready to use. Shake again before pouring over spinach and salad ingredients.

Simone Clements   **Bret Harte High School, Altaville, CA**

QUICK CAESAR SALAD

Makes 4 servings

1 head Belgian endive
1 small head romaine lettuce
½ small red onion, cut into rings

bottled caesar salad dressing
prepared croutons

Julienne endive, slice romaine leaves crosswise into ½ inch wide strips. Place endive, romaine and onion into salad bowl; just before serving, toss with dressing. Sprinkle with croutons.

Kathie Baczynski   **Mt. Carmel High School, San Diego, CA**

CHICKEN IN WINE WITH SAUTEED MUSHROOM SAUCE

Serves 6 to 8

Chicken:
8 to 10 boneless, skinless chicken
    breast fillets
flour seasoned with lemon pepper
    to taste
6 tablespoons oil
2 cups fresh mushrooms, sliced
butter or margarine for frying
1 can mushroom soup
½ cup chicken broth
½ cup orange juice

½ cup dry white wine (or vermouth)
1 tablespoon brown sugar
½ teaspoon salt
4 to 6 carrots, sliced julienne style
Sauce:
8 ounces fresh mushrooms, sliced
5 to 6 tablespoons butter or margarine
2 to 3 shallots, finely chopped
3 to 4 tablespoons Italian wine vinegar
    or red wine vinegar

To prepare chicken: Shake chicken fillets in flour seasoned with lemon pepper. Fry in oil until golden brown on each side. Fry mushrooms in butter or margarine. Combine remaining chicken ingredients in a large casserole dish or a 9" x 13" pan. Bake for 1 hour at 350 degrees.

To prepare sauce: Saute mushrooms in butter or margarine. In a separate pan, saute shallots in the wine vinegar. Combine the mushrooms and shallots. Serve with chicken.

Note: Serve with wild rice, a fresh green salad and pass the sauteed mushroom sauce.

"An elegant, easy dish! Serve on a platter with the carrots and garnish with fresh parsley. Tender and delicious. I adapted this from The Best of Bridge cookbook series."

Leslie Rodden   **San Gorgonio High School, San Bernardino, CA**

SHRIMP CURRY

Serves 4

½ teaspoon curry powder
1 cup mayonnaise
⅔ cup evaporated milk
1½ cups cooked shrimp

2 tablespoons green pepper, chopped
2 tablespoons pimento, chopped
1 tablespoon green onion, chopped

     Mother's Day

Blend curry powder into mayonnaise. Add evaporated milk and blend until smooth. Add rest of the ingredients. Heat, stirring occasionally, until thick and bubbly, about 20 minutes. Serve over hot, cooked rice.

"Very easy and fast to prepare. Not overly (curried) spicy, so most people like it."

Nancy Brunson　　　　　**McKinleyville High School, McKinleyville, CA**

CRAB AND AVOCADO CASSEROLE

Serves 4

2 ripe avocados
½ pound (2 cups) crab meat
3 tablespoons fresh lemon juice
salt
pepper

1 can cream of mushroom soup
1 cup dry bread crumbs
2 tablespoons butter or margarine,
*   melted*

Arrange sliced avocados and crab meat in alternate layers, sprinkling each layer with lemon juice and seasonings; in a greased 2-quart casserole. Pour the undiluted mushroom soup over the top. Mix crumbs with melted butter and arrange on top. Bake at 325 degrees for 20 minutes.

Inez Roberson　　　　　**Correia Junior High School, San Diego, CA**

PRALINE CASHEW CRUNCH

Makes 10 cups

1 (16 ounce) package Quaker Oat
*   Squares*
2 cups cashew pieces
½ cup honey

½ cup firmly packed brown sugar
¼ cup margarine
1 teaspoon rum extract
½ teaspoon baking soda

Heat oven to 250 degrees. Combine cereal and cashews in a 9" x 13" pan; set aside. Combine honey, brown sugar and margarine in a 2 cup microwaveable bowl. Microwave on high 1½ minutes; stir. Microwave on high ½ to 1½ minutes more or until boiling. Stir in rum extract and baking soda. Drizzle over cereal mixture. Stir to coat evenly. Bake 1 hour, stirring every 20 minutes. Spread on baking sheet to cool; break into pieces.

"This is a deliciously wonderful gift for little ones to make (with some help) for Mommy, Grandmommy, Godmommy and...one batch makes two nice gifts. Give in jars or cans that the kids can decorate along with a copy of the recipe. They'll be so amazed that they could make something that tastes so good. (Make sure they give more than they eat!)"

Patricia Sellers　　　　　**Morse High School, San Diego, CA**

The Whole Enchilada, Page 113

Hearty Healthy Chicken Salad, Page 136

MY MOM'S BEST DIVINITY

Makes 1 pound

2½ cups sugar
½ cup light corn syrup
¾ cup water

1 egg white + a pinch of salt
1 teaspoon vanilla
1 cup walnuts

In a medium saucepan place sugar, corn syrup and water. Cover and bring to a boil. Do not stir. Boil 2 minutes. Remove cover and cook until mixture reaches 238 degrees on a candy thermometer (or soft ball stage). Remove from heat. Let rest for 5 minutes.

Beat the egg whites and salt until stiff. Pour syrup into egg whites in a slow, steady stream, beating vigorously. Flavor with vanilla and adds nuts. Beat until it loses its "shine". Drop by spoonfuls on waxed paper. Allow to cool completely.

"Heavenly light and smooth! Worth the extra effort. Makes a great 'little' dessert for Mother's Day."

Priscilla Burns　　　　　　　　　**Princeton High School, Princeton, CA**

MOM'S FAIL-PROOF LEMON MERINGUE PIE

Serves 8

9" baked pie shell
1 package lemon pudding & pie
　filling mix
1 lemon
1 tablespoon butter

1 tablespoon cornstarch
3 egg whites
6 tablespoons sugar
pinch of salt

Bake and cool pie shell.

Prepare pudding mix as directed. When thickened, add juice and rind of lemon and butter. Pour into pie shell. In a saucepan, dissolve cornstarch in ½ cup (scant) cold water. Cook, stirring to boil and thicken. Cool completely. Beat egg whites until fluffy. Gradually add sugar and pinch of salt. Beat until thick and glossy. At low speed, add cornstarch mixture until blended.

Heap meringue onto hot pie filling; spread over filling carefully, sealing meringue to edge of crust to prevent shrinking or weeping. Bake at 350 degrees or until meringue is a delicate brown. Cool away from draft. Dip knife in water before cutting to prevent meringue from shrinking.

Janis Christopher　　　　　　　　**Mt. Whitney High School, Visalia, CA**

PERFECT PIE CRUST

Makes 5 pie crusts

*4 cups flour, lightly spooned
    into cup*
1 tablespoon sugar
2 teaspoons salt

1³/₄ cup shortening
1 tablespoon white vinegar
1 large egg
¹/₂ cup water

Mix flour, sugar and salt. Add shortening and cut in until mixture is crumbly. In a bowl, beat together the vinegar, egg and water. Pour liquid into flour, stirring with a fork until moistened and comes away from edge of bowl. Divide dough into 5 portions. Pat into flat ovals, wrap in plastic or waxed paper and chill. May be frozen. It never gets tough. Just thaw and use!!

I am sharing my 90 year old mother-in-law's pie crust recipe. It just does not fail and is always ready for you."

Sue Blass   **Valhalla High School, El Cajon, CA**

NEVER FAIL MERINGUE FOR PIES

Makes enough for 1 pie

1 tablespoon cornstarch
2 tablespoons cold water
¹/₂ cup boiling water
3 egg whites

dash salt
6 tablespoons sugar
1 teaspoon vanilla

Blend cornstarch and cold water in a microwave safe dish. Add boiling water. Microwave on MEDIUM-HIGH until clear and thickened. Cool completely.
Beat egg whites until foamy. Add salt. Gradually add sugar. Beat on high until stiff peaks form. Turn to low speed; add vanilla. Gradually add cold cornstarch mixture. Beat well on high for 10 minutes. Spread on a baked pie and bake at 350 degrees for 10 to 15 minutes.

"This meringue won't weep, water or wilt."

Jan Hirth   **Saddleback High School, Santa Ana, CA**

AHHH'S TRIPLE LEMON CHEESECAKE

Serves 20

1 Package SuperMoist lemon cake mix
¹/₂ cup flaked coconut (optional)
¹/₃ cup soft butter or margarine
3 eggs
*2 (8 oz.) packages softened cream
    cheese*

³/₄ cup sugar
1 teaspoon grated lemon peel
2 cups sour cream
¹/₄ cup sugar
*1 (22 oz.) can lemon pie filling (or you
    can substitute instant pie filling)*

Heat oven to 350 degrees.

Beat cake mix, coconut, butter and 1 egg in large bowl on low speed until crumbly. Press lightly in ungreased oblong pan, 13x9x2 inches.

Beat cream cheese, 2 eggs, ¾ cup sugar and the lemon peel until smooth and fluffy. Spread over cake mix and bake until set, 20 to 25 minutes.

Mix sour cream and ¼ cup sugar until smooth. Spread over cheesecake; cool.

Spread pie filling over sour cream mixture. Cover and refrigerate at least 8 hours.

My mother loves this because it's so lemony!"

Sue Nall   **Temple City High School, Temple City, CA**

FESTIVE HOLIDAY GIFT CAKE

Serves 8 to 12

1 (8 ounce) package cream cheese	*1½ teaspoons baking powder*
1 cup Parkay margarine	*¾ cup (8 ounces) maraschino*
1½ cups sugar	*cherries, drained and chopped*
1½ teaspoon vanilla	*½ cup pecans, chopped*
4 eggs	*1½ cups confectioners sugar*
2¼ cups all purpose flour	*2 tablespoons milk*

Heat oven to 325 degrees. Blend cream cheese, margarine, sugar and vanilla. Add eggs, one at a time. Gradually add 2 cups flour sifted with baking powder. Combine remaining ¼ cup flour with cherries and pecans; fold into batter. Pour into a greased 10" bundt pan or tube pan and bake for 1 hour to 1 hour, 20 minutes. Remove from oven. Cool 5 minutes then remove from pan. When cool, glaze with mixture of confectioners sugar and milk.

"For a festive Christmas touch, you can top the cake with red and green candied cherries."

Edna Nagami   **Carr Intermediate School, Santa Ana, CA**

ORANGE SPONGE CAKE

Serves 16 to 20

4 egg whites	*⅓ cup water*
4 egg yolks	*⅓ cup orange juice*
2 cups sugar	*grated orange rind*
2 cups flour, sifted	

Beat egg whites in a bowl with 1 cup sugar. (You must use an electric mixer and add sugar a little at a time.) Beat egg yolks in a separate bowl with 1 cup sugar. Add 1 cup of sifted flour to egg yolks mixing thoroughly. Add the ⅓ cup water to egg yolks and mix thoroughly. Add the second cup of flour, mix thoroughly. Add orange juice and orange rind, finish mixing. Fold egg whites into flour mixture. Bake in a greased and floured 9"x13" pan at 350 degrees for 25 to 30 minutes.

Frosting: Make a butter cream frosting substituting orange juice for your liquid. I also add orange rind to the frosting.

"Mom, thanks for the recipe. Birthdays weren't birthdays without your orange sponge cake with the 'dollup' in the center."

Renee Glennan   Sequoia Junior High School, Simi Valley, CA

MOM'S APPLE SKILLET CAKE

Serves 6 to 8

¼ cup butter	¾ cup sugar
¾ cup brown sugar	1 cup cake flour
½ teaspoon cinnamon	1½ teaspoon baking powder
4 cups apples (fresh or canned), sliced	1 teaspoon vanilla
½ cup walnuts	1 teaspoon salt
3 eggs	Whipped cream for topping (optional)

Melt butter in a 10 inch skillet; add brown sugar, cinnamon and mix. Spread evenly over bottom of skillet. Arrange apple slices on brown sugar and butter mixture and sprinkle nuts over apples. Beat eggs; add sugar and continue beating. Add flour, baking powder, vanilla, salt and beat smooth. Pour batter over apples in skillet. Cover and place over low heat. Bake about 30 to 35 minutes, until tender and done. When done, loosen edges of cake and turn upside down on large plate. Serve with whipped cream, if desired.

"I'm starting a new tradition in my family as of 1993 -- every Mother's Day from now on will include this delicious dessert on our menu."

Mary Springhorn   Anderson High School, Anderson, CA

GERMAN PANCAKES

Serves 6

½ cup margarine	1 cup milk
6 eggs	¾ teaspoon salt
1 cup flour	

Preheat oven to 400 degrees. Put margarine in a 9"x13" baking pan. Put in oven until melted. Combine eggs, flour, milk and salt. Beat until there are no lumps. Pour batter into hot baking pan. Bake at 400 degrees for 20 minutes. Serve with syrup, powdered sugar, fruit, etc.

"This is a favorite for weekends and holidays. It's quick and easy. It should look very lumpy when baked; as it cools it will collapse."

April Rosendahl   Chino High School, Chino, CA

BISCUITS SUPREME

Makes 10 to 12 biscuits

2 cups flour
4 teaspoons baking powder
2 teaspoons sugar
½ teaspoon cream of tartar

½ teaspoon salt
½ cup shortening
⅔ cup milk

Stir together flour, baking powder, sugar, cream of tartar, and salt. Cut in shortening until mixture resembles coarse crumbs. Make a well in the center and add milk, all at once. Stir until dough clings together. Knead gently on a lightly floured surface for 10 to 12 strokes. Cut with a 2½" biscuit cutter dipped in flour between cuts. Place on an ungreased cookie sheet and bake for 10 to 12 minutes at 450 degrees.

Antoinette DeNeve   **Charles D. Jones JHS, Baldwin Park, CA**

30 MINUTE SOUP FOR ALL SEASONS & TASTES (Potato Cheese Soup)

Serves 6

1 tablespoon oil
1 tablespoon butter
3 leeks (chopped white)
1 onion, finely chopped
1½ pounds red potatoes, peeled
    and diced
pinch of thyme

4 cups chicken or vegetable broth
1 cup light cream
1 cup milk
salt and pepper to taste
¼ pound Cheddar cheese, shredded
1 tablespoon cornstarch

Heat oil and butter in heavy soup pot. Add leeks and onion. Cook and stir until vegetables have softened. Add potatoes, thyme and broth. Simmer for 15 minutes or until potatoes are tender. Add milk and cream. Season to taste with salt and pepper. Heat slowly to a simmer. Carefully whisk in ¼-pound shredded cheese that has been tossed with cornstarch. Cook just long enough for cheese to melt.

Robin Ali-Christie   **Nevada Union High School, Grass Valley, CA**

POTATO SOUP

Serves 4

5 slices bacon
2 cups potatoes, diced
½ cup celery
½ cup onion, chopped
¾ to 1 teaspoon salt

¼ teaspoon pepper
½ cup milk
⅓ cup flour
3 cups milk

Father's Day

In large saucepan, cook bacon until crisp. Remove bacon from saucepan. Set aside. Add potatoes, celery, onion, salt, pepper and ½ cup milk. Bring to a boil. Reduce heat; cover and simmer ten minutes or until vegetables are tender. In a 1-quart jar with a tight-fitting lid, add flour to remaining 3 cups milk, shake well. Gradually stir into vegetable mixture. Cook over medium heat, stirring frequently, for 15 minutes or until thickened (do not boil). Garnish each serving with crumbled bacon.

"A great way to warm up on a cold day."

Melody Mayfield   **Las Plumas High School, Oroville, CA**

SPAGHETTI SAUCE

Serves 16

4 pounds ground beef
¼ cup oil
6 tablespoons onion, minced
2 (15 ounce) cans tomato sauce
2 (12 ounce) cans tomato paste
1½ cups water
1 tablespoon garlic, minced

2 teaspoons salt
3 teaspoons black pepper
½ cup sugar
6 tablespoons chili powder
2 tablespoons vinegar
1 teaspoon rosemary
½ teaspoon basil

Brown beef; drain. Add remaining ingredients and simmer 6 to 7 hours.

"This recipe comes from my favorite spaghetti house in West Virginia."

Nancy Hunyadi   **Fullerton High School, Fullerton, CA**

PIZZA CASSEROLE

Serves 6

1 (4 ounce) package pepperoni, sliced
1 medium onion, chopped
⅓ cup butter
6 ounces thin spaghetti
1 (8 ounce) can tomato sauce

1 cup (4 ounces) Swiss cheese, grated
1 pound Mozarella cheese, thinly sliced
6 mushrooms, sliced
½ teaspoon oregano
½ teaspoon basil

Boil pepperoni for 5 minutes; drain. Sauté onion in ⅓ tablespoon butter. Boil spaghetti for 10 minutes; drain and rinse. Melt remaining butter and spread in an 11"x7"x2" casserole dish. Toss with cooked spaghetti. Cover with tomato sauce. Layer in order listed: ½ Swiss cheese, ½ pepperoni, ½ Mozarella, mushrooms, onions, oregano and basil. Repeat layers of cheese and pepperoni. Cover and bake at 350 degrees for 25 minutes.

Liz Coleman   **Oroville High School, Oroville, CA**

OKOBOGI CHICKEN

Serves 8-10

3 cups cooked rice
3 cups cooked chicken breast, cut up
2 to 3 cans cream of chicken soup
$^1/_2$ cup mayonnaise
1 cup celery, chopped
1 tablespoon lemon juice

8 ounces water chestnuts, sliced
1 tablespoon grated onion
3 hard cooked eggs, chopped
1 cup corn flakes, crushed
$^1/_2$ cup sliced almonds
2 tablespoons butter, melted

Spread rice in a 9"x13" pan, then spread chicken over rice. Mix the soup, mayonnaise, celery, lemon juice, chestnuts, onion and eggs and spread over chicken and rice. Mix corn flakes, almonds and butter together and sprinkle over top of casserole. Bake at 350 degrees for 40 minutes.

"This recipe was given to me by a neighbor, Tricia Radmacher. It was given to her from relatives in Iowa and gets its name from a lake in the northeastern part of the state. This is very tasty and is easy to prepare ahead and freeze.

Linda Heinbach   **Yosemite Union High School, Oakhurst, CA**

LEMON HERB GRILLED CHICKEN

Serves 4

1 to 1$^1/_4$ pounds chicken pieces
$^3/_8$ cup vegetable oil
$^3/_8$ cup lemon juice
1 teaspoon seasoned salt

1 teaspoon paprika
1 teaspoon sweet basil
1 teaspoon thyme
$^1/_2$ teaspoon garlic powder

Place chicken in plastic bag or bowl. Combine remaining ingredients; pour over chicken. Cover or seal. Marinate in refrigerator several hours or overnight. Broil or grill chicken 4 inches from heat source for 15 to 20 minutes per side or until done. Baste often with marinade.

"This is a great tasting barbecued chicken--just make more marinade for more chicken."

Ronda Johnson   **Santiago High School, Garden Grove, CA**

POTATO FILLING

4 potatoes
1 onion, chopped
2 sticks celery, chopped
4 slices bread, torn or cubed
1 cube margarine

2 eggs
milk (enough to moisten)
seasoning to taste
parsley, finely chopped to taste

Cook potatoes in salted water, drain and mash. Sauté onion and celery until tender; brown bread crumbs in margarine. Add eggs and milk. Add egg mixture, onion mixture and seasoning to potatoes and mix well. Turn into a greased casserole; sprinkle on parsley and bake for 1 hour at 350 degrees, until lightly browned.

"My husband, Chuck, is from Pennsylvania and comes from strong German heritage. One of his favorite dishes comes from his mom, Pauline, one of the best cooks in his hometown of Schuylkill Haven. She has shared this wonderful potato filling recipe with me. It's a great variation on regular mashed potatoes."

Linda Heinback   **Yosemite Union High School, Oakhurst, CA**

CHOCOLATE CHIP MACADAMIA NUT COOKIES

Makes approximately 6 dozen 3"-4" cookies

2 cups margarine, softened	*4 to 4¼ cups flour*
1 cup brown sugar, packed	*24 ounces chocolate chips*
4 eggs	*¾ cup macadamia nuts, coarsely*
2 tablespoons vanilla	*chopped*
2 teaspoons baking powder	

Cream together margarine and brown sugar. Beat in eggs and vanilla. Stir in baking powder and flour. Stir in chocolate chips and nuts. Drop by spoonfuls onto lightly-greased baking sheets. Bake at 350 degrees for 10 to 12 minutes.

Becky Oppen   **Dana Hills High School, Dana Point, CA**

CHOCOLATE-BANANA CAKE

Serves 8

unsweetened cocoa powder	*½ cup butter, softened*
(for dusting pan)	*1 cup brown sugar*
1¼ cups flour	*2 eggs*
½ cup unsweetened cocoa powder	*1½ cups bananas, mashed*
1 teaspoon baking powder	*(about 3 cups)*
½ teaspoon baking soda	*1½ cups chocolate chips*
¼ teaspoon salt	*powdered sugar*

Preheat oven to 325 degrees. Butter a 6-cup bundt pan and dust with cocoa powder. Sift dry ingredients into a bowl. In another bowl, cream butter. Add brown sugar and beat until fluffy. Beat in eggs and blend for 2 minutes. Mix in dry ingredients alternately with mashed bananas. Fold in chocolate chips. Pour batter into pan and bake about 70 minutes.

Leilani Neiner   **Fontana High School, Fontana, CA**

SPICED PUNCH

Serves 6

1 (20 ounce) can pineapple juice
1¾ cups water
2 cups cranberry juice
1 teaspoon whole cloves

1½ teaspoon whole allspice
3 sticks cinnamon, broken
¼ teaspoon salt
½ cup brown sugar

Place pineapple juice, water, cranberry juice in the bottom of a coffee pot. Put cloves, allspice, cinnamon, salt and brown sugar in coffee basket. Plug in and let it go until it stops perking. Serve in small cups with a stick of cinnamon and a cookie.

"Very easy...and good!"

Gage Hewes   South Pasadena High School, South Pasadena, CA

CHOCOLATE COVERED FROZEN BANANAS

Serves 12

12 firm, ripe bananas
1 (12 ounce) package semi-sweet
    chocolate pieces

6 tablespoons salad oil
chopped nuts

Cut peeled bananas in half crosswise. Impale on wooden skewers and place in freezer for one hour or until thoroughly chilled. (Coatings will run off if fruit is at room temperature.)

Melt chocolate in top of double boiler over hot (not boiling) water. Add oil and stir until smooth. Keep warm over hot water while dipping.

Remove bananas from freezer a few at a time. Dip and roll banana in melted chocolate topping, making sure all surfaces are completely covered. Shake or twirl banana before removing from pan to remove excess coating. While coating is still soft, roll the banana in chopped nuts. If coating becomes too hard to hold decorations, apply a little warm coating to back of nuts and hold in place until it sets. When covering sets, place bananas on squares of foil, wrap securely and store in freezer until ready to eat.

Jane Van Wagoner   Walnut High School, Walnut, CA

BAKED FARM CHEESE

Serves a group

Farm Cheese:
1 pound cream cheese, softened to
   room temperature
½ bunch fresh basil, finely chopped
½ bunch fresh parsley, finely chopped
1 tablespoon dry oregano
½ teaspoon freshly ground black
   pepper

Tomato-Basil Sauce:
6 fresh whole tomatoes, scored,
   stems removed
1 tablespoon olive oil
1 tablespoon garlic, minced
¼ cup white wine
salt and pepper to taste
½ bunch fresh basil, coarsely chopped

Cheese: combine all cheese ingredients and set aside.

Sauce: Blanch the tomatoes in boiling water for 2 minutes. Remove from heat and immediately immerse in ice water. Remove skin and discard. Core and quarter the tomatoes. Drain most of the juice and reserve (if needed to add back). Heat the oil and sauté the garlic until lightly browned. Add the wine and reduce for 1 minute. Add the tomatoes, salt and pepper and continue cooking for 15 minutes. Remove from heat and add the fresh basil.

Preheat broiler. Ladle the sauce onto an ovenproof serving platter. Shape the farm cheese into a round, flat patty. Center the cheese on top of the sauce and broil 5 to 10 minutes until browned. Serve with garlic toast triangles.

"This recently acquired recipe is a family favorite. Because of the red color, it is especially attractive for Christmas Open Houses and 4th of July celebrations."

Karen Talley   **Santa Maria High School, Santa Maria, CA**

TERIYAKI WINGS

Serves a large group

¼ cup margarine, melted
1 cup soy sauce
¼ cup brown sugar
1 teaspoon dry mustard

¾ cup water
20 chicken wings, with tips cut and
   divided in half, or chicken
   drummettes

Combine all ingredients except chicken wings. Pour mixture over chicken wings and marinate 24 to 48 hours in refrigerator.

Spread chicken onto aluminum foil wrapped jelly roll pan without marinade.
Bake at 350 degrees for 1 hour, turning several times.

"I usually double or even triple this recipe, and I have served it at many parties and receptions. Everyone compliments the taste!"

Doris L. Oitzman   **Victor Valley High School, Victorville, CA**

PEACH NUT BREAD

Makes 1 loaf

1 cup dried peaches
$^{1}/_{2}$ cup water
$2^{1}/_{2}$ cups flour
$3^{1}/_{2}$ teaspoons baking powder
1 teaspoon salt
$^{3}/_{4}$ teaspoon cardamom

$^{1}/_{3}$ cup butter or margarine, softened
$^{1}/_{3}$ cup sugar
1 egg
1 cup milk
$^{1}/_{2}$ cup walnuts, chopped

Cut peaches into small pieces. In a small saucepan, combine peaches with water; bring to a boil and simmer 3 to 4 minutes. Set aside to cool. Sift together flour, baking powder, salt and cardamom. Cream together butter and sugar; beat in egg (mixture will appear slightly curdled). Blend in flour mixture alternately with milk. Stir in peaches and walnuts. Turn into a greased 5"x9" loaf pan. Bake at 350 degrees about 60 minutes or until a toothpick comes out clean. Let stand for 10 minutes, then remove from pan.

"I love peaches! I pick them in the summer and freeze them to eat in the winter!"

Jeri Drake Lane   **Canyon Springs High School, Moreno Valley, CA**

BLUEBERRY SALAD

Serves 12 to 16

2 (3 ounce) packages grape Jello
1 cup boiling water
1 large can crushed pineapple,
    drained (juice reserved)

1 can blueberries, drained
$^{1}/_{2}$ cup pecans
1 (8 ounce) package cream cheese
1 cup sour cream

Dissolve both packages of Jello in 1 cup boiling water. Drain juice from pineapple; add enough water to juice to make 2 cups. Stir reserved juice into dissolved Jello. Add blueberries, pineapple and pecans. Chill until partially set. Blend cream cheese and sour cream. Into a 9"x13" glass dish, drop spoonfuls of thickened Jello alternately with cream cheese mixture. Run a knife in both directions through the mixture several times to make swirls. Chill until firm.

Ava Smalley   **La Puente High School, La Puente, CA**

TAPIOCA FRUIT SALAD

Serves 6 to 8

1 ($11^{1}/_{4}$ ounce) can Mandarin oranges
1 ($13^{1}/_{4}$ ounce) can pineapple tidbits
1 ($3^{1}/_{4}$ ounce) package tapioca
    pudding mix
1 cup orange juice

1 cup fresh or canned peaches
1 to 2 bananas, sliced and drizzled
    with 1 tablespoon lemon juice
1 cup grapes
$1^{1}/_{2}$ cups miniature marshmallows

Drain oranges and pineapple, reserve pineapple juice. Cook pudding mix in 1 cup orange juice and ½ cup reserved pineapple juice until thickened (approximately 6 minutes). Cool well. Add peaches, sliced bananas, grapes and marshmallows. Refrigerate until set.

NOTE: Keeps several days and bananas won't turn dark.

"This recipe came from my grandmother, Edna Unverzagt, who enjoyed making it into her nineties. It's a family favorite."

Kimberly Boyd   **West Hills High School, Santee, CA**

HEARTY HEALTHY CHICKEN SALAD

Serves 6   **Photo on Page 125**

1 broiler-fryer chicken, cooked,   *1 teaspoon salt*
  skinned, boned and cut into chunks   *½ teaspoon pepper*
1 cup small macaroni, cooked   *¼ teaspoon oregano /*
3 tomatoes, cubed   *1 cup chicken broth*
1 cup celery, sliced   *1 clove garlic, split*
½ cup sweet red pepper, chopped   *¼ cup wine vinegar*
3 tablespoons chopped spring onion
  greens

In large bowl, mix together chicken (while still warm), macaroni, tomatoes, celery, red pepper and onion greens. Sprinkle with salt, pepper and oregano. In small saucepan, place chicken broth and garlic; bring to a boil over high temperature and boil for 10 minutes or until broth is reduced to ½ cup. Add wine vinegar and pour over salad, mixing well. Chill until cold.

Per serving: calories 192, protein 22.5 grams, total fat 5.7 grams, saturated fat 1.53 grams, carbohydrates 12.1 grams, cholesterol 61 milligrams, sodium 603 milligrams.

National Broiler Council   **Washington, DC**

EASY CHINESE CHICKEN SALAD

Serves 8

1 package Top Ramen noodles   *¾ cup rice vinegar*
  (crushed)   *½ teaspoon pepper*
small package spice mix from   *1 head cabbage, chopped*
  Top Ramen   *2 green onions, chopped*
1 tablespoon sesame oil   *2 tablespoons sesame seeds*
2 teaspoons soy sauce   *½ cup sliced almonds*
2 tablespoons sugar   *1 cup chicken, cooked and shredded*

For dressing: mix spice mix, oil, soy sauce, sugar, vinegar and pepper together. Chop cabbage and onion and top with toasted sesame seeds, almonds, chicken and dressing mix. Toss all together with dry noodles before serving.

"Low fat and great for summer potlucks. Everyone always wants the recipe."

Miriam Johnson　　　　　　　　**Venado Middle School, Irvine, CA**

ARTICHOKE-RICE SALAD

Serves 6

1 (6 ounce) package chicken flavored　　*¹/₃ cup mayonnaise*
　rice mix　　　　　　　　　　　　　*4 green onions, sliced*
2 (6 ounce) jars marinated artichoke　　*¹/₂ green pepper, chopped*
　hearts　　　　　　　　　　　　　　*12 pimento stuffed olives, sliced*

Cook rice as directed, omitting butter. Cool in a large bowl. Drain artichoke hearts; reserve marinade. Cut artichokes in halves and combine with mayonnaise. Mix rice with artichoke marinade, then add onion, green peppers and olives. Toss artichoke hearts with rice mixture. Chill.

"This is a quick salad, and it tastes great!"

Linda Brayton　　　　　　　**Grace Davis High School, Modesto, CA**

BECCA'S BROCCOLI SALAD

Serves 8 to 10

³/₄ cup mayonnaise or sour cream　　*1 medium red onion, chopped*
2 tablespoons sugar　　　　　　　　*1 cup sunflower seeds*
2 tablespoons vinegar　　　　　　　*¹/₂ cup raisins*
1 large bunch broccoli, raw
¹/₂ pound bacon, cooked crisp
　and chopped

In a large bowl, combine mayonnaise, sugar and vinegar. Cut broccoli into small pieces and add to dressing. Add bacon pieces, onion, sunflower seeds and raisins. Mix well and refrigerate. Serve the same day or next day--keeps well.

"This is a very refreshing crunchy salad. Has the best flavor if served the next day. Men like this salad."

Darlene Lupul　　　　　　　　**Tokay High School, Lodi, CA**

CHUCK WAGON BEANS

Serves 12

¹/₂ pound bacon slices　　　　　　　*1¹/₂ cup catsup*
3 pounds ground beef　　　　　　　*3 tablespoons prepared mustard*
6 medium onions, chopped (3 cups)　*1¹/₂ teaspoon salt*
1 cup celery, finely chopped　　　　*¹/₂ teaspoon pepper*
²/₃ cup beef broth (bouillon)　　　　*2 (1 pound, 13 ounces) cans*
1¹/₂ cloves garlic, minced　　　　　　*baked beans*

Fry bacon until crisp in Dutch oven or bean pot. Remove and drain. Pour drippings from pan. In same pan, cook and stir ground beef, onion and celery until meat is brown and celery is tender. Stir in broth and remaining ingredients; cover and bake 1 hour and 15 minutes or until hot and bubbly. Crumble bacon; sprinkle over beans.

"A hearty meal in itself. I usually serve it with potato salad, corn on the cob, and bacon wrapped cheese stuffed beef balls or hamburgers for a large gathering."

Ellie Wildermuth   **La Canada High School, La Canada, CA**

QUICK, HEALTHIER CHILI

1 large onion, diced	*1 teaspoon garlic powder*
2 medium green peppers, diced	*2 tablespoons chili powder*
3 tablespoons oil	*1 teaspoon salt*
1½ cups boiling water	*1 tablespoon sugar*
1½ cups TVP (textured vegetable protein)	*2 (14½ ounce) cans red kidney beans*
1 cup tomato sauce	*6 drops Tabasco sauce*
2 (14½ ounce) cans cut tomatoes	*pinch red pepper*

Sauté onion and green pepper in oil. Add remaining ingredients except kidney beans and simmer for 15 minutes. Add kidney beans and cook for 5 to 10 minutes more. Add more water if needed.

"You can sauté the onion and green pepper in water instead of oil to reduce the fat even more. Buy TVP at health food stores. It is a soy product and a great substitute for meat!"

Sally Spieker-Slaughter   **Tehachapi High School, Tehachapi, CA**

MARINATED GREEN BEANS

Serves 8

1 pound green beans	*¼ cup cider vinegar*
1 tablespoon salad oil	*2 tablespoons sugar*
1 small onion, thinly sliced	*1 teaspoon salt*
1 (4 ounce) jar pimento	*¼ teaspoon salad oil*

(Begin preparing this dish about 2½ hours before serving or early in the day.) In a 2-quart saucepan over high heat, heat 1" water and green beans to boiling. Reduce heat to low; cover and simmer 5 to 10 minutes or until beans are tender-crisp; drain and set aside. In same saucepan over medium heat, in 1 tablespoon hot salad oil, cook onion until tender, stirring occasionally. Drain pimentos, reserving 2 tablespoons liquid. Cut pimentos into thin strips; set aside. In a medium bowl with a spoon, mix vinegar, sugar, salt, salad oil and reserved pimento liquid. Add pimentos, cooked onion, and green beans; toss gently to coat with dressing. Cover and refrigerate about 2 hours to blend the flavors, stirring occasionally.

"Great to prepare ahead of time during the cool part of the day when the weather is hot."

Maridel Anagnos   **Tokay High School, Lodi, CA**

THREE BEAN CASSEROLE

Serves 6

4 to 5 strips of bacon, diced
1 medium onion, diced
1 (1 pound) can lima beans, drained
1 (1 pound) can red kidney beans,
   drained
1 (1 pound) can B&B Baked Beans

1 cup Tillamook or sharp Cheddar
   cheese, cubed
½ cup catsup
¼ cup brown sugar
dash Worcestershire sauce

Fry bacon and onion. (If using a crock pot, can be put in uncooked.) Add beans and remaining ingredients. Cook in crock pot for 1½ hours on high or in an oven at 350 degrees for 45 minutes.

"Every time I serve this recipe I get compliments from my guests."

Wanda Shelton   Newport Harbor High School, Newport Beach, CA

FRESH PEACH PIE

Makes 1 pie

1 cup sugar
3 tablespoons peach gelatin
2 tablespoons corn starch
¼ teaspoon salt
½ to 1 teaspoon almond extract

1 cup boiling water
6 to 8 medium-sized peaches, fresh
1 to 2 tablespoons lemon juice
1 9" pie shell, baked

In a saucepan, mix together the sugar, peach gelatin, corn starch, salt and almond extract. Add the boiling water and boil for 3 minutes; cool slightly.
Blanch, peel and slice peaches; toss with 1 to 2 tablespoons lemon juice. Arrange peach slices in pie shell. Pour cooled glaze over peaches and refrigerate until set.

Millie Deeton   Ayala High School, Chino, CA

FRESH FRUIT PIE

Serves 8

Crust:
1 cup flour
½ cup butter or margarine, softened
3 tablespoons sugar
¼ teaspoon salt
Filling:
1 cup water

1 cup sugar
3 tablespoons corn starch
3 tablespoons Jello (same flavor
   as fruit)
¼ teaspoon almond flavoring
4 to 6 cups fresh fruit (sliced peaches,
   strawberries, etc.)

Mix crust ingredients together and pat into a pie plate. Bake at 300 degrees for 20 minutes. Cool slightly.

Combine water, sugar, and corn starch in a saucepan and slowly bring to a boil. Stir in Jello. Add almond flavoring. Place prepared fruit in slightly cooled pie crust, pour Jello mixture over fruit and chill in refrigerator until filling is set.

"A favorite of family and friends. The crust is especially good when made with butter."

Irene Armijo   **Walter Johnson Junior High School, Las Vegas, NV**

FOURTH OF JULY PIE

Makes 1 pie

3 tablespoons corn starch	*¹/₂ pint red raspberries*
1 cup sugar	*1 pint boysenberries*
2 cups crushed strawberries	*1 pint strawberries, sliced in half*
1 tablespoon lemon juice	* lengthwise*
1 deep, 9" baked pie shell	*whipped cream or vanilla ice cream*
³/₄ pint blueberries	* for topping (optional)*

Prepare strawberry glaze by thoroughly mixing corn starch with sugar. Add crushed strawberries. Cook over medium heat, stirring constantly, until mixture is so thick it sticks to an inverted spoon. Stir in lemon juice. Cool until lukewarm before using. Spread a thin layer of strawberry glaze on the bottom of baked pie shell. Spread blueberries over the bottom. Spoon 3 to 4 tablespoons glaze over the blueberries. Spread evenly, then spread the raspberries, more glaze, the boysenberries, more glaze, then arrange the strawberries, cut side down, on top. Brush the tops of strawberries with remaining glaze. Chill the pie. Serve with whipped cream or vanilla ice cream on top.

"Bob Anderson created this pie. He wanted to use all the fresh berries of summer in one terrific pie."

Ramona Anderson   **Mira Mesa High School, San Diego, CA**

PEANUT BUTTER FINGERS

Makes 24 squares

¹/₂ cup butter	*1 cup flour*
¹/₂ cup sugar	*1 cup quick oats*
¹/₂ cup brown sugar	*6 ounces chocolate chips*
1 egg	*Topping:*
¹/₃ cup peanut butter	*¹/₂ cup powdered sugar*
¹/₂ teaspoon vanilla	*¹/₄ cup peanut butter*
¹/₄ teaspoon salt	*2 to 4 tablespoons milk*
¹/₂ teaspoon baking soda	

Cream butter; add sugars and cream well. Blend in egg, peanut butter, vanilla, salt and soda. Stir in flour and quick oats. Spread in greased 9"x13" pan. Bake 20 to 25 minutes at 350 degrees (325 degrees for a glass pan). Sprinkle with chocolate chips. Let stand for 5 minutes, then spread evenly over top.
Combine topping ingredients; mix well. Drizzle on top.

"Thank you, Lori, for this quick and easy midwestern family favorite. We've even made up a holiday as an excuse to make these!"

Robin Jongerius   **Jordan High School, Long Beach, CA**

STRAWBERRY CAKE

Makes 1 9"x13" pan

*1 package strawberry Jello
   (I use sugar-free)
1 pint fresh strawberries, cut up*

*OR 1 small package frozen
   strawberries, defrosted
1 angel food cake (torn up into pieces)
1 (12 ounce) carton Cool Whip*

Mix Jello according to instructions. Add fruit. Let set for 30 minutes, or until soft-set. Add cake pieces and pour into a 9"x13" pan. Cover with Cool Whip (use as frosting). Place sliced strawberries on top for decoration.

"This is a 4th of July Pot Luck favorite. It's cool and refreshing, not filling and very easy."

Libby Newman   **West Valley High School, Hemet, CA**

MIAMI BEACH BIRTHDAY

Serves 10

*6 ounces (1 cup) chocolate chips
1 cup flaked coconut
1/3 cup butter, melted
1/2 cup walnuts, chopped
2 cups flour
1 teaspoon baking soda
1 teaspoon salt*

*1/2 cup butter
1 1/2 cup + 2 tablespoons sugar
1 cup heavy cream
2 eggs
1 teaspoon vanilla
1 1/4 cups buttermilk or sour milk*

Preheat oven to 350 degrees. Grease and flour two 9" cake pans. Melt 1/3 cup of the chocolate chips. Combine coconut and 1/3 cup melted butter, stir in walnuts and remaining chocolate chips; set aside. Combine flour, soda and salt. Cream 1/2 cup butter in a large mixing bowl. Gradually add 1 1/2 cups sugar and cream until light and fluffy. Add eggs, one at a time, beating well after each addition. Blend in melted chocolate and vanilla. At slow speed, add dry ingredients alternately with buttermilk.

Mix well after each addition. Pour into pans and sprinkle with reserved coconut-walnut crumb mixture. Bake for 30 to 40 minutes, until cake springs back when touched in center. Cool. Beat remaining 2 tablespoons sugar with cream until stiff. Fill and frost layers keeping crumb side up during frosting.

"This is a family favorite from Christmas buffets to 4th of July and birthdays! Works great to make cake ahead, freeze; thaw out, then cover with whipped cream!"

Karen Talley   **Santa Maria High School, Santa Maria, CA**

ZUCCHINI CAKE

Serves 10

3 eggs	*2 teaspoons baking soda*
2 cups sugar	*1 teaspoon baking powder*
1 cup oil	*2 teaspoons cinnamon*
3 teaspoons vanilla	*¾ cup raisins*
2 cups zucchini, finely grated	*1 cup walnuts, chopped*
2 cups flour	*cream cheese frosting (optional)*

Combine eggs, sugar, oil and vanilla. Beat until smooth. Add zucchini and stir to combine. Sift together flour, baking soda, baking powder, and cinnamon. Add raisins and nuts to dry ingredients. Stir dry ingredients into zucchini mixture. Pour into a greased and floured 9"x13" pan. Bake at 350 degrees for 30 to 35 minutes. Frost with cream cheese frosting, if desired.

"A great use for our garden fresh zucchini and even the non-zucchini eaters in the family enjoy this cake on the 4th of July."

Judith Huffman   **Mariposa County High School, Mariposa, CA**

OLD FASHIONED "HOMEMADE" ICE CREAM

Serves 10 to 15

5 eggs, beaten	*1 to 2 bags ice*
2½ cups sugar	*½ package (2 to 3 cups) rock salt*
½ pint heavy whipping cream	*electric or hand turned ice cream*
1 quart half & half	*freezer*
approximately 6 cups whole milk	

Beat eggs until well beaten. Add sugar, a little at a time. Add whipping cream and continue beating. Then, slowly add half & half. Pour into ice cream freezer and finish filling ¾ full with whole milk. Cover. Put into ice cream freezer bucket, then put ice and rock salt layered around ice cream. Plug in or hand turn for approximately 30 minutes until ice cream is frozen. Pack in fresh ice and salt for about ½ hour to harden and serve.

Nancy Kappe   **Ranch Verde High School, Moreno Valley, CA**

OREO ICE CREAM

Makes approximately 4 quarts

4 eggs
2¼ cups sugar
5 cups milk
4 cups half & half

4½ teaspoons vanilla
½ teaspoon salt
24 Oreos, broken into fourths

Beat eggs and sugar well. Add milk, half & half, vanilla and salt. Mix well. Add Oreos. Freeze in ice cream freezer.

"This ice cream is chocolatey with chunks of cookies. More or less cookies can be added. Thank you, Margie, for another great recipe!!"

Cheryl McDaniels   **Green Valley High School, Henderson, NV**

PEACH CUSTARD ICE CREAM

Makes 1½ quarts

3 large eggs
2 tablespoons flour
1½ cups sugar
2 cups milk
2 cups peaches, peeled and coarsely
   chopped

2 tablespoons lemon juice
1½ cups whipping cream
1 teaspoon vanilla

In a large bowl, beat eggs. In a 3-quart pan, whisk flour, 1 cup sugar and milk until smooth. Stir often over medium heat until boiling, about 8 minutes. Whisking rapidly, pour hot sauce into eggs. In a blender, puree peaches with lemon juice and ½ cup of sugar. Stir into cooked mixture and chill, covered, until cold (about 1½ to 2 hours). Stir in cream and vanilla. Freeze in a 1½-quart (minimum) ice cream maker. Serve when soft.

"The only flavor of homemade ice cream the family knew about in the crestline cabins."

Sue Waterbury   **San Luis Obispo High School, San Luis Obispo, CA**

"POTTED PLANT" CAKE

Serves 6 to 8

8 ounces cream cheese
½ stick margarine
1 cup powdered sugar
3½ cups milk
2 small packages instant chocolate
   pudding

12 ounces whipped topping
20 ounces "Oreos" crushed
Gummi worms

Combine cream cheese, margarine and powdered sugar. Mix milk, pudding and whipped topping and add to first mixture.

In a large 12" flower pot (new), line bottom with crushed "Oreos", put in mixture, hiding gummi worms in mixture. Put crushed "Oreos" on top.

Garnish with plastic or silk flowers, gummi worms and a trowel for serving. Refrigerate until ready to use.

"Your guests will think this is a potted plant. Won't they be surprised when you serve it for dessert? Perfect for any summer get together."

Christine Ringenbach   **Rancho High School, North Las Vegas, NV**
Brenda Umbro   **Orange Glen High School, Escondido, CA**

LIGHT CANADIAN CHEESE SOUP

Serves 4

2 cups potatoes, diced	*1/4 cup reduced calorie margarine*
2 small carrots, diced	*3 cups nonfat milk*
2 small celery stalks, diced	*1/4 cup flour*
1 cup water	*1/8 teaspoon pepper*
1 chicken bouillon cube (low-salt)	*8 ounces Velveeta light, cubed*

Place in a large saucepan: potatoes, carrots, celery, water, bouillon and margarine. Simmer until potatoes are tender. In a small bowl, blend milk, flour and pepper. Add to saucepan and simmer until hot. 20 minutes before serving, add cheese cubes. Continue heating until cheese melts. Blend and serve.

Note: This may be slow cooked all day. If you add the cheese too soon -- it will look "grainy" but tastes fine.

"I 'lightened' this recipe. You can 'fatten' it up with regular margarine, Velveeta and milk."

Sharon Bennetts Jenkins   **Pinacate Middle School, Perris, CA**

ROSALIE'S RED CABBAGE SALAD

Serves 8

1 head red cabbage	*4 teaspoons wine vinegar*
3/4 (8 oz. bottle) "Wishbone" Italian	*pepper*
dressing	*season salt*
5 teaspoons sugar	

Core and shred red cabbage. In a salad bowl, mix together cabbage, dressing, sugar and wine vinegar. Season to taste with pepper and season salt. Refrigerate one hour before serving.

"A nice addition to any barbeque. This recipe was created by my Aunt Rosalie and loved by all who try it."

Katie Placido   **Warren High School, Downey, CA**

SPINACH TORTELLINI SALAD

Serves 4 to 6

*1 bunch spinach, cleaned with stems
    removed*
*2 cups cheese tortellini, cooked
    and cooled*
*1/2 pound bacon, fried crisp
    and crumbled*

1/2 cup green onion, diced
1 cup purple cabbage, shredded
cherry tomatoes, as desired
1 cup "Hidden Valley" ranch dressing

Layer ingredients in an oblong pyrex dish. Start with spinach, then tortellini, bacon, green onions, cabbage and tomatoes. It can be made in advance and dressing poured over just prior to serving.

"I got this recipe from my favorite sister-in-law."

Angela Cruz-Trujillo   **Valley View High School, Moreno Valley, CA**

VEGETABLE STUFFED POTATOES

Serves 4 to 8

4 large baking potatoes
*1/2 head fresh broccoli (or 10 oz.
    box frozen chopped broccoli)*
*1/2 head fresh cauliflower (or 10 oz.
    box frozen cauliflower)*
1 medium onion
1 clove garlic, crushed

2 tablespoons butter
8 oz. reduced fat cream cheese
parmesan cheese, freshly grated
1 cup reduced fat sour cream
salt and pepper to taste
*1 1/2 cups medium Cheddar cheese,
    grated*

Scrub potatoes well and poke holes in tops to prevent exploding while cooking. Bake in microwave 15 to 20 minutes or until tender (some microwaves take longer than others and time varies with size of potatoes). Meanwhile, cook broccoli and cauliflower until crisp and tender (if frozen, cook and drain well). Cut broccoli and cauliflower into small pieces. Saute onion and garlic in butter. When potatoes can be easily pierced with a fork, cut in half lengthwise. Carefully remove potato from shell. To the pulp, add sauteed onion and garlic, creamed cheese, parmesan cheese and sour cream. Mash until fluffy. Add salt and pepper to taste. Carefully stir in desired amount of broccoli and cauliflower. Fill each half shell with the mixture and top with grated Cheddar cheese. Reheat in microwave until cheese melts. Serve immediately.

Sharon Turner   **El Dorado High School, Placentia, CA**

ALPHABETIZED CONTRIBUTORS' LIST

AAA

Agee, Vicki, 17
San Marcos HS, San Marcos

Ali-Christie, Robin, 129
Nevada UHS, Grass Valley, NV

Alley, Lynn, 34
Diegueno JHS, Encinitas

Anagnos, Maridel, 138
Tokay HS, Lodi

Anderson, Ramona, 140
Mira Mesa HS, San Diego

Anderson, Marion, 19
A. G. Currie MS, Tustin

Apple, Cheryle, 21
Rio Vista HS, Rio Vista

Armijo, Irene, 140
Johnson JHS, Las Vegas, NV

Atkin, Anna, 16
Monache HS, Porterville

BBB

Baczynski, Kathie, 20, 123
Mt. Carmel HS, San Diego

Bankhead, Marilyn, 18
San Marcos HS, San Marcos

Banks, Judy, 63
Temecula Valley HS, Temecula

Banicevich, Gerry, 37
Cordova HS, Rancho Cordova

Batchelor, Linda, 109
Hesperia HS, Hesperia

Becker, Trena, 71
Ball JHS, Anaheim

Beigle, Karen, 51
Villa Park HS, Villa Park

Bender, Carol, 28
C. K. McClatchy HS, Sacramento

Bennett, Karen, 102
Norco HS, Norco

Betz, Judy, 25, 62
Greenfield JHS, Bakersfield

Black-Eacker, Ellen, 121
Nogales HS, LaPuente

Blanchard, Julie, 56
Western HS, Anaheim

Blass, Sue, 126
Valhalla HS, El Cajon

Bleecker, Laurie, 23
Chino HS, Chino

Blohm, Rita, 6
Nogales HS, La Puente

Blough, Shirley, 59
Hillside JHS, Simi Valley

Bohte, Nancy, 12
So. Pasadena HS, So. Pasadena

Bowman, Cindy, 97
McFarland HS, McFarland

Boyd, Kimberly, 135
West Hills HS, Santee

Bradley, Amber, 33
Granite Hills HS, El Cajon

Brayton, Linda, 49, 137
Grace Davis HS, Modesto

Bressler, Barbara, 14
Buena Park HS, Buena Park

Brown, Darlene, 66
Golden Valley MS, San Bernardino

Bruce, Libby, 42, 101
Troy HS, Fullerton

Brunson, Nancy, 124
McKinleyville HS, McKinleyville

Buckley, Signe A., 64
Moore MS, Redlands

Buhman, Carol, 102
Fountain Valley HS,
Fountain Valley

Burke, Brenda, 58
Mt. Whitney HS, Visalia

Burkhart, Nanci, 112
Hueneme HS, Oxnard

Burnham, Jill, 74
Bloomington HS, Bloomington

Burns, Priscilla, 125
Princeton HS, Princeton

Byrne, Betty, 23
Vaca Pena MS, Vacaville

CCC

Call, Carole, 22, 33
Costa Mesa HS, Costa Mesa

Campbell, Theresa, 60
J.F. Kennedy HS, La Palma

Campbell, Sue, 26
Chico JHS, Chico

Carr, Mary, 49
Enterprise HS, Redding

Carriere, Julie, 92
No. Monterey HS, Castroville

Castro, Diane, 100
Quartz Hill HS, Quartz Hill

Childers, Penny, 71
Ramona HS, Ramona

Christopher, Janis, 125
Mt. Whitney HS, Visalia

Contributors

Mitzenmacher, Jeannette, 102
Antelope Valley HS, Lancaster

Molinaro, Adriana, 74
Helix HS, La Mesa

Montelongo, Tricia, 112
South JHS, Anaheim

Montoy, Joanne, 50
Esperanza HS, Anaheim

Moody, Deanne, 36
Monte Vista HS, Spring Valley

NNN

Nagami, Edna, 127
Carr IS, Santa Ana, CA

Nall, Sue, 127
Temple City HS, Temple City

Neiner, Leilani, 132
Fontana HS, Fontana

Nelson, Rhonda, 45
Warren HS, Downey

Newman, Libby, 141
West Valley HS, Hemet

Niadna, Penny, 105
Golden West HS, Visalia

OOO

Oitzman, Doris L., 134
Victor Valley HS, Victorville

OKeeffe, Alice, 54
Walnut HS, Walnut

O'Keefe, Carol, 56
Canyon HS, Anaheim

Oliver, Jan, 2, 15
Irvine HS, Irvine

Oppen, Becky, 132
Dana Hills HS, Dana Point

Oxford, Sally, 12
Monache HS, Porterville

PPP

Panttaja, Virginia, 81
Sanger HS, Sanger

Paskins, Linda, 108
Cordova HS, Rancho Cordova

Paul, Nan M., 99
Grant MS, Escondido

Pearl, Vicki, 22
Giano IS, La Puente

Pearson, Susan, 78
Lincoln HS, Stockton

Pendleton, Susie, 3
Cerritos HS, Cerritos

Peters, Cindy, 87
Park JHS, Antioch

Pierre, Jan, 25
Cabrillo HS, Lompoc

Pius, Bonnie, 119
Sanger HS, Sanger

Placido, Katie, 144
Warren HS, Downey

Policy, Janet, 65
Ramona HS, Riverside

Priestley, Roberta, 2
Alhambra HS, Alhambra

RRR

Ranger, Beverly, 4
Carpinteria HS, Carpinteria

Rayl, Charla, 33
Fallbrook HS, Fallbrook

Rector, Mary M., 108, 111
Valley HS, Las Vegas, NV

Redman, Anita, 64
John Muir MS, Burbank

Richmond, Mary, 86
San Luis Obispo HS,
San Luis Obispo

Riness, Janet, 52
Westminster HS, Westminster

Ringenbach, Christine, 144
Rancho HS, No. Las Vegas, NV

Roberson, Inez, 124
Correia JHS, San Diego

Robinson, Linda, 97
Royal HS, Simi Valley

Rocha, Ruthanne, 37
South Fork HS, Miranda

Rodden, Leslie, 123
San Gorgonio HS,
San Bernardino

Roe, Gaylen, 72
Magnolia JHS, Chino

Rohm, Susan, 77
Cimmarron HS, Las Vegas, NV

Rosendahl, April, 128
Chino HS, Chino

Ross, RoseMary, 13
North HS, Bakersfield

Rupp, Jackie, 53
Home Street MS, Bishop

Rupp, Michael A., 101
Live Oak HS, Live Oak

Russo, Ginger, 79
Chico JHS, Chico

Ruth, Lynda, 9
La Mirada HS, La Mirada

SSS

Sack, Rhonda, 45
Home Street MS, Bishop

Salau, Loretta, 5
Foothill HS, Bakersfield

Sarouhan, Olga, 110
Edison HS, Huntington Beach

Contributors

Winzenread, Linda, 51
Whittier HS, Whittier

Wolff, Carol, 120
Desert Springs MS,
Desert Hot Springs

Woodall, Cora Lynn, 53
Green Valley HS, Henderson, NV

Woolley, Linda, 52
La Sierra HS, Riverside

Worland, Janet, 72
Silver Valley HS, Yermo

YYY

Yonter, Kathleen, 81
Burkholder MS, Henderson, NV

ZZZ

Zallar, Sue, 41
Capistrano Valley HS,
Mission Viejo

Contributors

INDEX OF RECIPES

Holiday Cooking For All Occasions
California Cookbook Company
1907 Skycrest Drive
Fullerton, CA 92631

Please send_____ copy(ies) of your cookbook at **$9.95** each (includes tax and postage). Make checks payable to: *California Cookbook Company.*

Enclosed is my check for $_____ .

Name_____

Street_____

City_____ State_____ Zip_____

Holiday Cooking For All Occasions
California Cookbook Company
1907 Skycrest Drive
Fullerton, CA 92631

Please send_____ copy(ies) of your cookbook at **$9.95** each (includes tax and postage). Make checks payable to: *California Cookbook Company.*

Enclosed is my check for $_____ .

Name_____

Street_____

City_____ State_____ Zip_____

Holiday Cooking For All Occasions
California Cookbook Company
1907 Skycrest Drive
Fullerton, CA 92631

Please send_____ copy(ies) of your cookbook at **$9.95** each (includes tax and postage). Make checks payable to: *California Cookbook Company.*

Enclosed is my check for $_____ .

Name_____

Street_____

City_____ State_____ Zip_____
